THE THOUGHT THINKER
IS A LONER GIRL

Teen Anxiety, Drug Use, and Existential Discontent

J. GUZMÁN

Introduction

On Being is a meta case study. It is a case study that becomes
aware of itself as a case study. **It is essentially the archived,
written record of the evolution of my consciousness** (I am
your protagonist Ana), and it will continue until my
inevitable death. It encompasses my projections, my
fantasies, my life experiences, my ego contradictions and
self-awareness pirouettes corkscrewing into the Ether. It is
darkly meta poetry, my Shadow, my Stockholm-Syndromatic
love notes to Saturn, a Plutonian tunneling into fear, anxiety,
hatred, jealousy, unhappiness, self-loathing, negativity, pride.
It is an exploration into who and what I am. It is my suffering
transformed into art.

OB is a work of Time, and I dedicate it to those with the tools
and knowledge to interpret it. One of its primary purposes is
to aid in the exploration of astrological knowledge. Astrology
is the study of cyclical, energetic patterns in Time, and *OB* is
a documentation of a particular moment of Time (my birth)
unfolding, evolving, and maturing throughout Time. I have
provided many years of dates and the personal experiences
and events that correspond to them, as well as my (Ana's)

birth info. Any clever astrologer can analyze the data provided – the 'so below' – and make symbolic and literal connections with celestial movements – the 'as above.' Thus *OB* serves as raw data for metaphysical analysis, and ideally it will stimulate intellectual discussion concerning a variety of astrological concepts and timing techniques.

I intend on analyzing the astrology of *On Being* myself, but at the time of this writing I'm still very much a novice. I am currently pondering the logistics of said analysis. All I can say is that with Time and *OB*, I will show you how astrology works. However, you'll also need to do your own research and analyze critically what I/Ana say/s. We are the Unreliable Narrator. Our thoughts are tricksters, just like the most famous psychopomp itself.

How can one know anything is real, trapped inside her own mind, perspective, context, birth chart? We are embedded in context and can never be free. *OB* is an example of this, as it deals with internal, subjective truth, as opposed to external, objective Truth. It is personal experience, emotions, feelings, thoughts, ideas. It is a wholly idiomatic perspective, not one solely involving concrete Fact.

The characters in *OB* are real people, with their names and physical characteristics altered to protect their identities. It is not meant to slander or condemn, only to convey a personal psychological evolution, which inherently involves contact with the Other, and naturally results in various emotions about said contact. (And obviously I'm gonna talk shit about you in my diary).

For this reason *OB* straddles the line between fiction and nonfiction. It is neither, yet both. It is not memoir, it is not an autobiography. It is not literary fiction, or a coming-of-age novel with a wonderfully stereotypical story arc informing you that it'll all be okay in the end and everyone finds love. *On Being* is a case study, a fool's experiment in self-awareness, an exploration of beingness. It is my lifelong dissertation on Divine Energy.

I must explore my own consciousness, use words to outline its endlessly changing structure, hide it and fight it and let it oppress me. *OB* is a vast, psychic structure functioning as my 12th house prison, safe house, bunker, cage. It is my Saturn remediation, the spider-webbed contours of my psyche, my attempt at grabbing the slippery, eel-like form of intuition and Knowing without words. How can I catch Energy with words? How can I put into words that which is inherently a fleeting image, a flash of feeling, a nonlinear system functioning as part of a larger system, gyrating into Infinity? The size scale is limitless, the parts all cooperate and are themselves made up of smaller parts.

I want to be your favorite psychonaut architect, both your slave and your master, your lover and muse, a strange, ephemeral ghost inside your head, someone you can project your fears and desires onto. I want you to talk about me when I'm there and not there. I want you to use me for metaphysical, psychological, astrological research. I want you to cut me open, delve into my depths, point out patterns and idiosyncrasies and blind spots. I want you to show me how it all works systematically, how it's all connected, a grandiose, energetic clockwork ticking away into the Abyss, fate and free will two lovers at a house party, sipping whisky and sharing a joint, an occasional cigarette, coffee in the morning.

I want you to judge me, pick me apart, comment on my thoughts and opinions, mock me, hate me, obsess over me, emulate me. Ultimately, this isn't for you. Fuck you. Fuck the audience, this is for *me*. I must anchor myself in the present moment by dealing with my suffocating, negative emotions through writing. *On Being* was only a byproduct of this process, until I became aware of that perfect synergy of science and spirituality, called astrology. Now *OB* has a larger, more meta purpose, but I will always use it as a tool for greater self-awareness.

I need it for my sanity, for my continued personal growth, for the preservation of my memories. I need it, or I become lost in despair and confusion and apathy. I need it, or else I can't figure out what's real. Without it I cannot understand who I am and why I exist. (Am I only startled movement in a broken mirror? An uncomfortable, inverted image? A black-and-white shadow of the truth? A faint whisper of dream-memory? A shimmering, indefinite question left unvoiced?)

Without *On Being* everything is meaningless to me.

I need it, you don't. That's why I say it isn't for you. Maybe it can help you untangle your own mess of a mind, but I am not writing it *for* you – as, for example, genre fiction or podcasts are made principally to please an audience. If I'm writing for anyone other than myself, it is for the astrologers, but it is not meant to solely please them. It is meant to make clearer their symbolic, archetypal language by exposing an inner truth connected to Time.

(Everything will become clearer with Time. How can I please you, my lord? Words are spells, my lord, and you have me spellbound.)

I will admit that at first I did think I was writing for you – or rather, publishing for you. As the reader, it's your money I'm earning. But I realized I will do this regardless of whether it earns me money (which, incidentally, I'm sure is the key to success and happiness – working hard at something you'd do either way). So I began to forget about you. I appreciate you, but you are not the Purpose.

When putting together the first three books I had you in mind. I made extensive edits so that it would be easier for you to read. I made sentence structure clearer and more linear, I made the grammar more formal. I removed many parts I saw as boring, and added clarifying information to parts that didn't seem to convey wholly the emotion felt at the time of the initial writing. Thus books 1-3 are highly edited, and subsequent books won't be. (Although I will obviously still do edits.)

I have come to a greater understanding of why I am writing this, publishing this, exposing to you my Shadow. I hope it can help you in some way, but it's really meant to help *me*.

J. Guzmán
June/July 2021

p.s. The location from where Ana is writing is usually clear (a necessary data point for the astrological analysis). However, book one often doesn't specify the location, and when it doesn't it was probably written in Meridian, ID, her home base. (Just an aside for the astrologers.)

for astrological purposes

❧

Ana Ebtz
14 January 1991
8:42 a.m.
Lewiston, ID, USA

The Thought Thinker is a Loner Girl
(first publication, eBook version)
22 March 2020
9:46 a.m.
Meridian, ID, USA

❧

un mensaje del futuro

❧

"Tu tiempo vendrá.
Ya sabes que eres el absoluto."
-J. Guzmán

❧

THE THOUGHT THINKER IS A
LONER GIRL

19 March 2007

Two days ago I smoked mota for the very first time, from a
bong made out of a chocolate milk jug by Sawyer, my older
brother. Is he corrupting me, or is he teaching me? Either
way, I feel he is being the older brother he should be.

The makeshift bong was to be immersed in water in the
kitchen sink. You push the jug down into the water while
burning the herb, and use the pressure to collect all the smoke
together at the top so that you can suck it out and inhale it all
from a hole in the top. It was weird, but I bet I could recon-
struct it.

In reality, I didn't like the feeling that came after. I just felt
delayed and vaguely forgetful. I remember feeling something
between fear and anxiety while I was getting ready in the
bathroom. I heard Sawyer tell his friend in the living room
that Mom was coming home in five minutes and it made me
really anxious.

Turned out he was just fucking with us and she wasn't going

to be home for a few hours. That made me feel even more anxious because I realized how bad I was freaking out in my mind over nothing.

Anyway, smoking mota doesn't seem that bad to me, like it is stereotyped to be. I think everything seems so ominous if you've never tried it, but once you do, you realize how stupid and not a big deal it is. Unless it's, like, meth, I guess.

25 March 2007

I think I try to define myself too much, and when I can't I get in a bad mood. I'm always trying to see myself from other people's perspectives instead of my own, and I think it makes me uncomfortable. I think I should just live my life.

I hope there is no such thing as reincarnation because I think I am the only person I would want to be. I always imagine being other people and living in their shoes, and it makes me happy that I'm me, or depressed for them because I know I wouldn't want to be them.

It's kind of complicated, but sometimes I think of other people imagining they were me and feeling depressed for me because they are glad they aren't me. Just like how I think of other people. It makes me feel depressed or sad or uncomfortable. I'm not exactly sure how it makes me feel, but not good.

01 April 2007

I was thinking about how I always watch people around me and I have my own thoughts and observations about them. And I thought about what other people think when they see me. I always feel kind of invisible because I never catch people looking at me; it's like they never do. I also thought about how I see people and wonder who they are and why they are there and their life histories and all their feelings about everything.

I'm not the type of person to ask someone who she is. I don't know what I'd say if someone asked me who I am.

20 April 2007

Whenever I'm talking to someone, like at school, I often find myself tongue-tied or trying to find the right words to say, but just screwing them up and saying something that doesn't make sense or is really dumb and boring. And it makes me so anxious. While it's happening I think about how I have to say something or they'll think I'm weird and can't talk. I hate this.

20 May 2007

I finished my book today and I realized that every book makes me feel the same. Upon finishing I feel empty and sad, like I'm missing out on a part of life that is essential to my being. That's the only thing I hate about books: the emptiness at the end.

I wish my life could be as surprising and enigmatic as the ones I read about. I wish certain events could change me and shape me, mold me into the person I am today. But, I guess they do. All sorts of things happen to me, I suppose.

Maybe if I wrote about my life and the people I interact with, others would feel the same way I do after I finish reading a novel. Maybe all of our lives are like this. Maybe everyone's life is exciting and influential to some degree, but each person takes life for granted and does not notice or enjoy what she has. I dunno. I just feel like nothing interesting ever happens to me.

15 June 2007

Dad and I rented the movie *The Fountain*. It was perfect. It was about life and death. About how life is only a fraction of being, leading up to death. It was insanely good.

16 June 2007

Sometimes I get weird feelings about life. Like living it in a certain, preferable way. Like never wearing shoes and living in your bikini. Or the sandy beach hair I wish I had, or doing homework in coffee shops. Having conversations with bed-headed, real, nice boys in coffee shops, and riding bikes downtown. Living downtown. Rain forests, plants, everything being green.

Every time I imagine living with or around these things, I get really pleasant vibes. I want to be the people that encompass these vibes. I want to be the actual activity described. I can't explain the feeling.

I wish I lived in a city right on the beach, on the top floor of a skyscraper in a tiny apartment with a balcony or rooftop like a jungle, with plants everywhere. When I think of this I get the feeling. "The Feeling." I would ride my bike everywhere: to work, to the beach, to the grocery store where I would purchase magazines and hair dye.

When I think of Pike Place Market I get The Feeling. I'm having a hard time explaining The Feeling. It's like every-thing is perfect in a rolled-right-out-of-bed way that is so not perfect. I love it, but I can't explain it. It's just intensely

4

authentic and genuine to me. Oh, and wearing a lot of bracelets, and riding longboards! Those trigger The Feeling also.

26 June 2007

I wish I could debate. I wish I could thoroughly explain my thoughts, express my feelings to a great extent without coming across as an ignorant cretin. My peers frustrate me because they don't see things the way I do. They don't understand that there is something more, that people are fragile and real and that life is pretty.

I wish people in films were real, because the movies I watch that completely inspire me, that portray life in the way I feel is right and true, make me feel like I belong to that lifestyle where things are messed up and imperfect, sheltered inside a beautiful world. This is a place where people are serious, a place where people have real problems to overcome, a place where I want to be.

And when the film is over, I turn to see people so unlike the characters I adore, people I don't want to be around, people that frustrate me. They aren't real and don't give a shit about the fragility I sense in everything. Meaningless. I wish I could find someone similar to the movie's characters.

I want to create something beautiful and inspirational, something I can belong to and feel proud of. I want to travel and experience new cultures, maybe because I want to find someone different.

06 July 2007

I decided that I'm a huge hypocrite, and that I'm wrong about

5

many things. My own opinions often feel wrong to me. That is irritating to me because opinions are not right or wrong. In terms of being a good or bad person, maybe they are. To the majority of people good and bad are clearly defined, but I suppose that is also an opinion. This matter frustrates me because there is no answer. Everything is seen differently through the eyes of each individual.

I often feel like I can't write what I'm thinking, or describe things well. I'm worried about putting everything into complete sentences and having it make sense. But life doesn't make sense. I will now write whatever comes into my head, without worrying about it.* I don't care about it being beautiful, logical, right. It will simply be.

[*Ana: Do just that. And don't worry, I'll edit it for you so that it's perfect. –J.]

I always try to analyze myself. I think of all the opinions and statements that could be thrown at my writing, me, who I am, and I try to talk about them. I feel so passionate about finding out about myself and who I am, but I'm always frustrated because I can't figure it out. I don't know what to look for.

I decided I'm very interested in the afterlife.

My characteristics contradict each other. I'm mismatched, hypocritical. My insides have opposition. I'm open minded, but I don't give people a chance. I'm bitter and resentful, but forgiving and kind. I'm calm but nervous and worried. I like busy and loud places, and calm and quiet places. I especially like when those places exist when united.

07 July 2007

I think it's interesting to read things from the past. To

remember your own experiences, or to learn of someone else's past life. What were they doing while you were sleeping? While you were off in your own world, completely unaware of their hardships and glorious victories? Maybe that's why I take the time to write in here. To be able to look back on this in years to come and remember a past personality. To savor my tiny glimpse in history.

02 August 2007

Jenna and I got into this ridiculous argument about what porn is, because I showed her a picture of a naked woman (you couldn't see anything) in a fashion magazine, and she freaked out and claimed that it was porn. I said, "Our bodies are beautiful. That's not porn, you can't even see anything." And she stated, in this annoyingly passionate voice, "Yes it is! Our bodies are not for show and tell!"

She is my Mormon next-door neighbor that I've known since I was one and she was two. My first friend. She is petite with brown hair and is always in love with someone at school. I grew up with her, and it's really quite unfortunate for her because I'm basically the antichrist.

God, she is so fucking close minded. A naked person is not porn. A naked person doing disturbing things to himself or others is porn. Why can she not learn to love the human body, to see that to be nude is to be beautiful, and that skin is pretty and that it's not a terrible thing to see?

I was super frustrated today about her determined argument that anything baring skin is pornographic. She seriously needs to be liberated. I thought about that scene from *Titanic* when he's drawing her as she's laying nude on the bed, and how romantic that is. I don't think Jenna's even seen that movie because her parents have brainwashed her into thinking that it's porn and evil.

21 August 2007

I wish everyone would recycle, and think about life and people and why things are the way they are. I wonder if it's in my nature to constantly look for some way to be different, to set myself apart from others. The things I think about are mine alone. If everyone thought about these things I would just want to rebel in some way. I wonder if I'd like it if the world at large had the same interests as me, or if I'd despise it and thrash the world in an attempt to not be a clone.

06 October 2007

Trust, friendship, finding one person that you'll love for the rest of your life, regret, the beautiful stranger that you'll never know, being misunderstood, being alone, honesty, writing down everything, learning something new all the time, reading, having an open mind, restraints, flying, living, lying, sleeping, wishing, wanting.

25 November 2007

I'm on an airplane from Los Angeles to Boise. I was at a soccer tournament. This is what I see outside my window: a gray-blue dream world illuminated by a circular white moon. Darkness is almost a burden on its pure complexion. The clouds are not clouds; they are fields of cotton, miles of mountainous white lumps, silvery wisps clumped together in slumber. A multilayered universe shielding a completely different, electric world.

Sometimes I feel like I say things to people only because they want me to say them. I feel like I don't care about anyone. I speak because they are talking to me and I can't just sit there unresponsive. My reply is basically what I assume they want to hear. I don't really know what I'm trying to say. I just don't want to talk to anyone anymore, only to myself.

When I'm most naturally myself is when I'm alone. I don't need to adjust to anything. I can talk to myself and not feel stupid or embarrassed about what I say. Like right now, as I'm writing this, I feel most myself because I'm just writing down my thoughts. I don't need to worry about anything, just talk, because no one is going to read this. Writing makes me feel most naturally myself.

At the same time, that whole paragraph makes me kind of uneasy because I don't think I explained myself very well. You see, I don't talk about things that are actually truly important to me with anyone. I don't think anyone would understand. I don't know why. Usually, when I'm talking to people at school, I don't give a shit about them, or what they're interested in, so I just give them what they want to hear.

Maybe I'm a loner. And I'm most myself when I'm with myself.

14 December 2007

Lately I've felt super annoying. I can't explain it well because I don't fully understand it. It's kind of like when I was talking about how I only say things because people want me to say them. It's like these things pop out of my mouth sometimes and I can't suppress them and then I feel stupid. Like, I can't take myself seriously. And if I can't, no one can. I think at soccer practice I'm really annoying, too. God! This is so frustrating.

Lately I've been lonely? Depressed? I dunno. It's like I can't decide if I want to be around people or be alone, and I think the best thing for me right now is to get a lot of rest and be by myself for a while.

Writing all this out made me feel much better I think. I like that. It's weird. Once I write it down I figure everything out and get my thoughts organized, and then I'm able to give myself advice. Once I see it on paper I can make logical conclusions.

27 December 2007

I've been thinking about how slowly time goes by, but in movies or books they can summarize a person's life or a long event, like a pregnancy, in 30 seconds. It makes me feel really weird and uncomfortable, like everyone is ignoring how long everything takes.

When I read these types of summaries I try to pause after a statement like "three years later" and reflect on the past three years of my life, and realize how much I've changed and how much has happened to me in that time period. I'm super strange.

29 December 2007

Sometimes I wish someone would find my diary somewhere and read it and relate to me…and be a real person. And contact me, and return it, and know me. It's complicated. It's just that I can't willingly give my diary to someone to read, because it's so private.

I absolutely hate being vulnerable with anyone, and that's what would have to happen. I'd have to lose it or something so I wouldn't be giving it to someone on purpose. But the right person would have to find it! And shit like that never happens to me. Fuck.

03 January 2008

I feel like many different people combined. I have this idea where I want to be everybody at once. I feel this to be true sometimes. I react to other peoples' personalities with something from my own, to complement theirs, if that makes sense. I'm easy going so I change according to everyone else, and what they seem to want from me I give them. I'm a chameleon. But I don't mean that I won't disagree with someone or stand for what I believe in or be different.

08 January 2008

Today I had many feelings that confused me. First of all, I felt like I hated everybody. One thing that I do a lot, but I try not to do (but I still do it anyway) is imagine what it would be like to be a certain person in one of my classes. I always manage to become very depressed, because I pick apart her appearance and what she says until I can't stand her. Then I wonder if my classmates do the same thing to me, and I start to think about all the negative things in my life.

I feel like there is some universal opinion on life, clothes, attitudes, or lifestyles that I am not included in. Everyone is normal and boring and has the need to be popular (whatever that means), and I often feel as if I need to be this way, for no apparent reason. I know I will never be this way and that is good, in my opinion.

But that's where the universal opinion comes in. Everyone thinks the same way, but I don't, so I think I'm wrong or bad, or something. Now I'm just confusing myself. I'm starting to hate everyone, but I hope those words never escape my mouth. I'm serious though, I really cannot stand school.

In Spanish class today this super smart girl presented her project with her group, and she memorized, like, all of it, and she just acted so cool and collected up there. For some reason I hate her so much. Usually, I hate the stupid kids, but I realized that I also hate the smart kids, too, because they aren't interesting to talk to.

They just focus on what is correct and right and they don't embrace life, the dirty parts of life, I mean. Like getting into trouble or smoking mota, or feeling like shit, or not doing your assignments and realizing that it's not a big deal.

I think that everyone should laugh and have fun and the smart kids don't understand that, and I thought they, of all people, would, for some reason. Like this girl named Tracy. She's a complete idiot because she's rude and only focused on being intellectual and not being friendly.

For speech class we did persuasive speeches, and mine was about how homosexuality is not a choice, and that it has biological and cultural influences. (It's evolution, baby.) At the end of it when it was time for questions, Tracy asked me with this rude tone, "So why is it not natural?" All I said was, "It is natural!" I wanted to say that perhaps it isn't normal in our bullshit society, but it is natural, as a biological phenomenon that occurs in the world.

But I didn't say anything; I felt too flustered. Then I felt angry at myself for not having some great retort that would put her in her place.

And I get so pissed at myself because when I do find someone that is interesting to me, I never know what to say to them, and I just mess things up or act boring! I felt stupid today after school because I was walking down the stairs with River, and he's always super funny and I'm so not funny, and I couldn't think of anything to say, so I was dumb and boring.

River is into fashion. He is tall and judgmental but in a funny, sarcastic way, and he makes fun of everyone, including himself, and watches fashion shows. He always has something witty to say, and my responses are lame as fuck. Usually I laugh because I don't know what else to do. Anyway, I was wearing high heels too, so I walked down the stairs really awkwardly. All in all my day sucked.

I feel like I need to go do something bad because life is bad and I'm a teenager and I should be taking risks. Why can't I take risks? I wish I could be reckless, and truly feel it, but I can't. It makes me too anxious.

09 January 2008

Today I felt very irritable. And tired. Dad has been annoying me lately. First of all, when I'm writing my emails to college soccer coaches, he tells me to change my sentence structure so it will sound better when I'm telling a coach that my grandma stayed with us for two weeks during Christmas break. I mean, is a college coach seriously going to analyze how I organized that sentence? Probably not!

I'm emailing college coaches in an attempt to form some kind of relationship with them, so that I may be able to go to their school and play on their team after I graduate high school. I

13

also might be able to get a scholarship with soccer so that school is less expensive. The whole thing stresses me out!

I feel fat and I eat too much food, too much food that isn't good for me, too much food in general. At least I have soccer tomorrow. I think the only reason I'm so tired is because I haven't been exercising. But it's only been, like, three days since our last practice, so I don't know why I feel shitty.

I hate school and I'm dreading it tomorrow. I don't want to be around everyone. I can't stand them anymore.

10 January 2008

Today was very…dynamic. School was the usual, shitty. I had an orthodontist appointment and when I got back to school I went through the back doors to get my ID card to sign in with, and since they were locked, I knocked on the door. And these kids were sitting there, and they looked at me standing there in the cold, rolled their eyes, and kept talking.

I was like, "Are you fucking kidding me?" I mean honestly, no one is that rude. I was furious. Finally one of them let me in, but the other, I hate him, just completely ignored me, and added an eye roll and a shake of the head. Seriously, I want to come to school with a knife and slit his throat. So after that I was in a bad mood for a long time.

13 January 2008

Last night I was eavesdropping on Sawyer and his friend talking about this book Sawyer is reading called *The Singularity is Near: When Humans Transcend Biology*. I admire them both because even though they like to get drunk and high and stuff, it's not all they do. They are interested in the world and reading and having adventures and intellectual conversations. That's the difference between them and all the idiots at school that do it because they think they are cool but don't know anything about anything.

I would like to be like Sawyer when I am his age, because to me he has a poetic personality. I mean, I'd like to be like that now, I guess, but I don't think I am. And anyway, he is six years older and that's a huge difference.

14 January 2008

Today is my birthday. I am 17 now. Sawyer drove me to school and picked me up. He got me this sweet Rage Against the Machine shirt that has nuns with guns on it.

At lunch Lisbet bought me breadsticks and we left school and smoked mota. She is short and blonde and also plays soccer. We play club soccer together and are both on the varsity team at school. She is someone that I consider to be cool, and one of my only friends.

Lately I've been thinking about how sometimes I get super overwhelmed with my existence. I think too many things, often all at once, and they get all mixed up inside my head and I can't sort them out, so I get immensely frustrated and confused.

Sometimes, in those moments, I'm thinking about the fact that I'm thinking, and then I try to sort out my facts and I can't. It's like when you can't do something when you're thinking too hard about it. You just have to do it, and it will work. Just don't try so hard.

I think that can often be the reason for suicide. I think certain people feel more strongly about life in general, more than other people, and when something doesn't work out, they are so passionately frustrated or confused, or angry, or over-whelmed. I am like that sometimes.

But I think I'm stronger than committing suicide. I get depressed because it's like circles and circles and never-ending shapes and whirls. Even thinking about killing your-self is weak so why don't you just do it?* I can't explain it. I guess I'm "emo."

Something else I've been thinking about is that I wish people would just know what I wanted, without me having to tell them. I mean, not completely. I think I want someone to know what I would like and do weird, creative things for me without me having to tell him.

I want someone to make me a movie, addressing me by name instead of as a passive audience member. Maybe I want someone to know how I'm feeling without asking me.

[*Um, please don't kill yourself. You are a physical manifes-tation of Divine Source! If you killed yourself you'd ruin the lives of your friends and family. Also, you'd probably just be reincarnated instantly and have to do everything over again, but in a shittier situation. Wait till your Saturn return is over, then decide. –J.]

24 January 2008

Today I got kicked out of lunch detention for talking. It's fucking stupid, at my school you get a lunch detention if you are late to class. Or if any teacher decides you deserve to have lunch detention. It's like a prison.

And they sit us down in the gym upstairs, everyone against the wall but right next to each other, like shoulder to shoulder.

How can you not communicate to someone sitting right next to you? Ugh.

I see lots of people in magazines, and they aren't real people. It's weird. I always wonder what the model's favorite things are, or what they were doing in their normal life at that exact moment that I saw them in the magazine, or how their personalities are, or where and how they grew up. I don't know these things, so they aren't real people to me.

25 January 2008

I was thinking, if you were schizophrenic, that state of being would be real to you. How could someone say that what you think is wrong, a mental disorder? I guess it would be different based on what the majority of people feel, but I dunno. For some reason it doesn't seem right to me for people to put others on medication because their state of being isn't the same as other people's state of being. I'm not sure, though.

Generally people are hostile to those that are different, those that are not considered normal. But normal is so boring! If you were schizophrenic, wouldn't you be more interesting? I wonder what it would be like, what it would feel like. What if they were happy? Would it be all right then?*

[*Ana: The thing is, they usually aren't happy. They take medication because their state of being is often extremely unpleasant and makes normal life difficult to manage, not because society says they are "wrong" or "bad." Yes, their experiences are very real to them, but they often prohibit the person from being able to function normally or complete simple tasks like getting dressed in the morning. –J.]

Eli and I saw *Into the Wild*. Emile Hirsch is beautiful. I feel like I looked up to him in that film rather than falling in love with him. Is that what love is?

Eli said he knew I would really like this movie. He's my best friend. We actually dated freshman year and he was my first kiss, but now we are just friends. He is good at soccer, like me, and has a white man afro. He is also on the guys' varsity team at school.

We argued at the end of the movie about the idea that happiness is only real when shared. I don't think I need anyone to be happy, but Eli does. I think maybe I will change my opinion someday.

I also think Eli is weirdly wise, but I am stubborn so I stick to my opinions and act independent and self-sufficient. I think I am both of those things, though. Also, Eli always gets that small smile like he's playing along with my childishness, and it makes me uneasy so I have to reassure myself. Anyway, I think I am a late bloomer, so…I dunno.

I'm distancing myself from Lisbet. Not in a super obvious manner because I don't want her to even realize it consciously, because I feel like that could create some dramatic thing that I don't want. But I think it would be a good thing for me to be around her a little less.

It seems like she's a bit pushy. She's stubborn like me, and believes that she is always right, and if I disagree with her opinions I'm stupid. Or bad, or just wrong. I think it's good for us to not be together all the time. Because she makes me feel really stupid a lot, and I hate that feeling. And she gets pissed when I don't want to smoke with her.

One time at school I said hi to this girl named Sadie that Lisbet doesn't like, because she thinks Sadie is full of herself and annoying, which she kind of is. But when she was gone Lisbet was like, "I can't believe you just did that! I can't believe you added her on Myspace! Don't talk to her! Blah Blah Blah!" I thought it was so dumb.

Because I am my own person, you know? I can acknowledge anyone I want, let me be me. It's not like Sadie is my best friend now. I've never even hung out with her before. And I still hang out with Lisbet the most. We are together a lot it seems like, at least at school, and we have soccer together all the time, so whatever.

04 February 2008

I had a weird day. After school I drove around for forever, and I felt like if I could just do that for eternity I'd be happy. No need to explain anything to anyone. Actually, I felt like I had been doing that for all eternity and had just then realized it.

I felt like I was the only one in the entire world left, although there were hundreds upon hundreds of streams of endless cars on all sides of me. I drove slow. I rested the back of my head upon the headrest and closed my eyes at stoplights.

The sun looked like summer. It always does on the Fairview and Cole intersection. I felt like I didn't have to go to school and it was warm outside. I was tired and hungry, but I was alive, and it was different. Alive in a slow, comatose way.

One of my recent acclaimed resolutions is to not say things I don't mean. I'm not going to tell people what they want to hear if I don't mean it. I don't know if I can accomplish this because I feel like I don't care about anyone. I feel like when I talk to people I simplify everything I say to them, because if I told them what I'm really thinking they wouldn't understand it or know what I'm talking about.

So I save a whole explanation about it and tell them something I don't mean, don't stand by, or don't care about. And when I say they don't understand me, I don't mean that I think I'm smarter or intellectually superior. I just think their reaction would be along the lines of, "What the hell are you talking about?" Like, I have difficulty explaining what I feel.

I feel like I'm supposed to have all these friends and go to parties and brag to everyone about getting hammered. But I don't want to. I want to be alone because there is no one that's real. I don't want to be pressured and I don't want to hear about things I don't care about, and I only want friends that feel things like I do, but there is no one.

Lisbet has Alyssa, who is a year younger than us and has been Lisbet's best friend since they were little, and Eli is a boy and is way more personable and social than me and I hate everyone he talks to. He has stopped inviting me to those high school parties because he knows I would rather sulk in my room than talk to any of those people.

Lisbet hates those people, too, but she has her own group of punk, stoner kids. I don't think her punk friends are very intellectual, though, which I feel is a required characteristic of a potential friend for me, even though I do like the punk mindset and fashion sense. Oh my god, I hate everything.

06 February 2008

Last night I went to the dollar movie with Sawyer. We snuck beer into the theatre and hard lemonade for me. Three, actually, but I only drank two of them that night. Then today at lunch I chugged the third in my car alone because I forgot my lunch and I figured that it would fill me up, and maybe make the insufferable sufferable for the rest of the day.

Sawyer has a lot of philosophy books that I want to read. I'm reading, like, five books right now. Mainly *The Subtle Knife* and *The Great Gatsby*, which are both very good, and then this Marilyn Monroe book and a book about Leonardo da Vinci, both on the side. And also bits and pieces of Sawyer's books and art books I have in my room.

Calculus test today, horrible. I'm sure I got a D or C-, at most. I'm incredibly frustrated right now. I have to register online for classes, read a shitload for my Spanish class, and my soccer coach wants me to call the fucking Utah State coach, when I really don't want to go to Utah State. I really don't want to go there. At all.

Tomorrow I have the second part of my Calculus test, which I'm sure will be even worse than today. I haven't studied. Maybe I won't, because I won't know what the hell is going on either way. This is stupid. I hate school so much. I don't care about Calculus; it's too hard and I have given up on trying to do my homework because my teacher doesn't grade it anyway.

It's 11:07 p.m. I better go to bed, I guess. I'm tired. I wish it were summer and all I had to do was lounge around and read and draw and write all day, every day. I'm worried about being out of shape for soccer. But actually it shouldn't matter, because colleges already want me and I won't be out of shape forever.

09 February 2008

I think a lot of people want to be everything and everyone, but maybe they don't realize it. Actors do, and writers, because they create something new and different, and there probably is a little bit of each of them in their work. I think I portray my lust for diversity mostly through fashion. And I love to read and watch movies and try new things, and I'm so inspired by everybody.

I copy people a lot. I do and say a lot of things I see other people doing and saying. Only if they are interesting though, and that doesn't include anyone I really know. I don't copy anyone at school because I hate everyone at school. It's mostly just artists or musicians that I look up to, or characters from movies or books that I love.

I have a lot of things to say sometimes, and nothing at other times.

18 February 2008

Yesterday Eli and I went to the movies. *Cloverfield.* It was cool, I guess. We snuck in the side door at the theatre and got in free, it was sweet! But we couldn't figure out what theatre it was in, so I asked the guy that takes tickets, and he told me right off the top of his head. He didn't even look suspicious of us. Basically we are like James Bond.

Eli and I always try to be super smooth and have adventures and be badasses, and I think James Bond is a good description of what we aspire to be.

22 February 2008

Yesterday I had no homework so I went night skiing with Sawyer and one of his friends. We smoked mota but I didn't really feel it. Sawyer left me and his friend alone in the cafeteria when he went to get our food, and it was terribly awkward! He asked me about going to university in Seattle, which is where I am leaning towards the most right now, and all I said was, "Yeah..."

Then it was silent, and I realized I probably should have elaborated a bit, like saying which school, exactly. But no, I do not know how to talk to people face to face. I shouldn't be worried about this, I guess, because there's nothing I can do now. I just felt stupid in that silent space, and I waited an inappropriately long time to be able to reply like a normal person, so I left it there.

I have a headache and when I close my eyes I feel like everything is turning around and around and around. I've been thinking a lot about suicide lately because we are talking about it in my health class. Not thinking about committing suicide, just suicide in general and reasons for it.

I think that for me, life is so indescribable and very overwhelming.

All I think about is why I am thinking what I'm thinking, and that I'm trapped in this body and I can't get out, and that no one understands anything I do, and that the things I can't understand are all right there in front of me and I can't grasp them, and wondering whether what schizophrenic people experience is real or not. I can't understand how that would feel or what it would be like.

I try to control my mind and it's too hard. I get all these furious random thoughts and I can't think them all through because there are too many, and I get so frustrated. The people I talk to aren't real, and I keep thinking about suicide and death and mental disorders. In a way, having one seems kind of appealing to me for some reason.

Being disturbed seems dark and mysterious. But at the same time, it scares me, and I wonder if I have some kind of mental disorder because I feel really irrational, and that scares me, too. I feel like I'm going to commit suicide even though I think I know I won't, but just thinking about it scares me.

Often, everything I have just written comes to me at once, and I feel helpless because my mind won't sort it all out because it's an information overload. I'm frustrated because I want someone to understand but no one is real and I can't find anyone that would understand. At the same time, I say in my head, why does human nature automatically entail the need for kinship and understanding and empathy? Why do I need that?

I try to push it all away and control my mind and not feel the need for it, but I find myself guiltily seeking a mutual understanding with another person. And no one's there. Also, I find it extremely difficult to speak to people, because everything I have to say isn't in order at all and I have to write things out or it gets all messed up. In fact, everything I've just said is all wound up inside of itself. I can't keep anything straight.

23 February 2008

I think that last entry was a panic attack. I was really tired and hungry and it was weighing down on me.

Eli and I went to the movie *Be Kind Rewind* last night. We snuck in again, so James Bond-like. It was fresh as fuck. And Mos Def is super attractive, oh my god. I'm also a little obsessed with his music. I love his song "Sunshine."

On the way home we passed this empty parking lot with a lot of trees, and in all the trees were hundreds of crows. It was peculiar because it was dark and the sky was lusciously purplish, and there was a huge mass of them there, looming against the deepening of the night. It was something I've never seen before. Mystifying.

There's this weird thing about me not thinking people are real. I'm starting to think that nobody is real. Like my friends and acquaintances, even family sometimes. Everything is starting to look so strange to me. Human bodies, fuzzy animals, fingers. It's too weird.

28 February 2008

My history class went to the Warhawk Air Museum and it was pretty cool. This one man I really liked told us, "There will always be wars because people are people." When Eli asked him if flying planes and shooting at people was intense, he said no. I'm glad he said that because Eli, and all other people including myself, don't seem to realize how terrible war is. It's not a game, it's not cool to be scared, so scared, always, and to pray that you don't have to kill anyone, to pray that you won't be killed the next day.

And I feel stupid saying that because I have no personal experience and don't understand it to any tiny degree, but it's probably true anyways.

03 March 2008

On Saturday we had two soccer games. The first I scored in. A good shot, actually. The second we lost but it was fun. I slapped this girl in the face when she wouldn't let go of my arm. I secretly felt like a badass. On Sunday we had one game and we won, but it was very slow and I was tired so it wasn't much fun.

Today is Monday, school wasn't too bad. I'm at the public library now, trying to get the rest of my homework done. I think I want to write a book. Maybe one day, when I have time.

In Health we are watching *Supersize Me* and it makes me never want to eat fast food again.* Whenever I eat I always think of starving people, and how fortunate I am to have what I have. It always makes me feel guilty and ashamed of myself for ever feeling sad or angry, because my life is infinitely better than many other people's. It always makes me very unhappy with the people around me. I begin to feel as if everyone is so greedy.

I feel naive and ignorant a lot of the time, and I want to change what happens to people that are starving or that live terrible lives. Like in Darfur. I don't really understand it, but I know people are being brutally killed there, and there isn't really anything that I can do about it.

[*Ana: Good. You shouldn't eat that shit. It's quite literally poison. –J.]

10 March 2008

Today I was thinking about how funny it is when people blink. I think it's hilarious! Because they have to, so it's like I can secretly command them to do it, and when they do it I laugh to myself. Also, it reminds me of butterflies and flowers and fragile things, and I like those thoughts.

I need to do my Calculus homework. I feel like I never get anything done, it's really frustrating. I feel like I'm in a whirlpool and I keep seeing the same assignments over and over and it's scaring me.

I was thinking about how we are all hypocrites. Society pressures us to be a certain way: clean, polite. It looks down on those that are not that way. However, in the solitude of our own homes, we all disobey society's demands. We are all hypocrites.

I dress the way I do because I am rebelling against a society that embraces conformity and a lack of individualism. Fashion is my rage against societal norms, my cry to the people to become individualists.

18 March 2008

I've decided that I am a genius. I had the coolest idea of writing something on the bathroom stall at school every time I go to the bathroom. I wrote "chaos surrounds me" today, and a poem I made up in fifth period about how I am everyone and everything. I thought it was cool. It gives me a kind of rush, as dumb as that sounds.

21 March 2008

Today is Friday and I'm at the public library. I escaped the school assembly today and got out, like, an hour before everyone else! It was tight. I totally James Bonded it, too. I snuck out of Calculus early and booked it down the stairs and out to my car. It was amazing.

It's kind of weird that I have to sneak out. It proves how prison-like my school is. Teachers guard the doors so that we can't escape during assemblies, because usually they are after classes are over so there is no point in staying.

24 March 2008

I watched *Rain Man* with Sawyer last night and it was terrible! I fell asleep during it, and slept on the couch for most of
the night until I got cold and woke up. The whole movie was
about Dustin Hoffman being annoying and Tom Cruise
yelling in an obnoxiously nasally voice at him. Lame.

30 March 2008

Sawyer and I drove to Lewiston to visit Grandma a couple
days ago, and he brought some "special" cookies for us to
enjoy on the five-hour drive. I ate two, didn't know they
were special until I ate, like, one and a half, and because I
have never had those before I didn't know how potent they
were. So after I finished the second one I got incredibly
sick.

After a while I realized I couldn't really feel my arms. Everything started rolling around and turning and spinning and I
couldn't open my eyes because it was too much. I started to
feel sick, and since we were still driving it made the spinning
way worse. When we got to Grandma's new house (which is
so nice and clean) I threw up all over her new carpet and
promptly went to bed. Oh my god.

My best friend slash cousin Camila came over to visit me but
we didn't get to hang out because I was sick and couldn't
even see anything. She has long, dark hair and light eyes and
fair skin, and I have always thought that she is really pretty.
She kept trying to bribe me out of bed and I was like,
"Camila, seriously, I am going to vomit everywhere if I
get up."

The funny thing is that we told everyone that I got sick from a gas station hot dog. I don't think I even told Camila that it was actually mota cookies.

31 March 2008

I made it through the school day. Surprisingly. It was the first day of the last quarter of my junior year of high school. Today was actually a pretty good day. At lunch Sawyer and I went to this little Mexican restaurant next to the pizza place we normally go to, since the pizza place doesn't take credit cards. It was delicious!

After school Mom and I took Sawyer to the airport to go back to Los Angeles. He goes to college there on a swimming scholarship and is about to graduate. He is probably going to live over there for a while after that before he figures out what he wants to do. His graduation ceremony is in May so we will probably drive down there for it.

I feel lonely sort of, as weird as that sounds. No, I don't think I'm lonely. I think I'm just a bit jealous that he's going to LA to chill with his friends and not go to school, while I get left behind in the middle of nowhere attending a jail-like high school, with no real friends. It's really quite depressing.

Sometimes, when we have company and I am dreading their departure, I'll close my eyes and pretend that they are already gone, back to their own homes, eating whatever they find in the cupboard, slipping into a familiar bed, even though they are actually in the room next to me, in an unfamiliar bed, eating the Cheetos I tried to hide from them.

I try to simulate the same empty feeling I get when they do leave, so that I may come back to a pleasant reality and sneak up next to them and sit, watchful, waiting to hear their stories, their experiences.

For some inexplicable reason I do this all the time, even when they are not actually in the room next to me, but somewhere far away. I always wonder what other people are doing. Like, I wonder what Camila is doing right now, or what Sawyer is thinking. I wonder if people ever think about me, if they wonder what I do on the weekends or what I'm thinking about during first period.

03 April 2008

Hey, random thoughts:

Lazy. What is the point of anything? Is there a reason we pursue knowledge, losing ourselves in libraries of mathematical equations, or proudly raising our hands when we know the answer? Why would I raise my hand if I don't get something in return? A candy, maybe, or a participation point. I know there have been times when I know what others don't, but I sit quietly waiting, because is informing everyone else of my knowledge really worth the effort of raising my hand?

I have spent a good deal of my time doing things that are futile. Useless. Is it because I am lazy that I consider them pointless?

Nostalgia and songs, songs that give me nostalgia.

In this universe are people who stand for something they don't know anything about. For a minute glimpse of mysterious reality no one understands. I can tell I am one of them by the way people look me up and down.

Alone isn't bad. The tone of your voice when you say it accuses it of ghastly crimes.

The girl in the back corner of the library with her mind folded quietly into the pages of her book averts her eyes when meeting yours.

The bathroom stall holds secrets of the mind of a revolutionary.

08 April 2008

Yesterday, when I was riding my bike home from the public library, I crashed and scraped my chin, hand, and knee, and it hurt. And I was embarrassed but I don't think anyone saw. Anyway, I have a scab under my chin now and I feel like a child.

I went to the orthodontist today and I got purple braces this time. I love going to the orthodontist because it means I am closer to getting my braces off. I cannot wait! That will probably be one of the best days of my life, I'm dead serious! I've had them since the beginning of high school and I feel like I will still have them when high school ends.

Soccer practice was cancelled today. I think that's a good thing because I'm pretty sore from my bike crash. I'm texting Eli about colleges right now. Maybe I should go to bed.

10 April 2008

Björk is my idol.

I want to be in college. Now. I am ready! But, maybe I'm not. I'm probably still immature. Whatever, I dunno.

I want to travel the world so badly. It's weird, but I feel as if I'm going to be in high school for eternity. I feel like I've already been in school for eternity, and I want a change. I want to experience new things, new places, new people. I'm super sick of being here.

My junior year is almost over. I have less than two months! After this month maybe school will be easy. I mean, I'll get more projects I bet, but Spanish will probably be a lot easier. I am excited for summer!

I should be a poet. And publish a whole bunch of shit from my diaries. Or just my whole diary. That would be kind of fresh. I guess.

14 April 2008

I decided this diary is boring and not very poetic.

I really like the grunge look.

I can't wait for summer. I cannot wait!

I'm at the public library. I'm going to rent *Being John Malkovich*. I'm so tempted to rent a book to read.

I have no inspiration for writing right now. Oh, I wrote on the bathroom wall today. I wrote: "Why erase the documentations of reality? The mind of a revolutionary is strewn across this wall." I came up with that all on my own, spur of the moment.

Basically, what I was thinking was that I'm annoyed when the janitors erase my thoughts and feelings that I give birth to. I give them to the people secretly, the stall is merely my method of transportation. I am a phantom, a silhouette of creativity. A vessel of little traces of inspiration, pure hope that I can one day create my own inspiration.

16 April 2008

Right now I'm emotionally unstable because the weather is fucking with my head, I feel like I'm wasting my day, soccer practice is at an inconvenient time, I miss my past, and I don't want to kiss boys. That is what I'm feeling right now. I dunno if what I'm missing is my past or just those carefree days in the summer sun.

20 April 2008

The past few days I was in Portland for a recruiting trip for soccer. I stayed in the dorms with a freshman on the team and it was really fun. She was cool; her hair was extremely short and curly and she had bleached a strip in the center blondish, like a mohawk. Her room was creative. I slept on the couch.

The first night I went on a campus tour, and I love their campus! I talked with an academic advisor and with the coach of the soccer team. Then that night in the dorms we played Guitar Hero and watched TV. The next day they had a game so we went to that, but they lost 2-0. It was kind of shitty. After that Mom, Dad, and I explored downtown Portland and ate dinner at a pizza parlor. We rode the tram, or trolley, or whatever it's called. It's free.

Then I went back to the dorms. They were having a birthday party at the soccer house, so we got all dressed up and wore high heels and I wore these ridiculously short shorts. When we got there we went upstairs and took shots of Absolut Vodka and talked with a soccer girl that had just graduated.

I got super drunk that night. I talked to a few random people. There were a ton of people there, and I met this wrestling recruit from Las Vegas named Glen. We hooked up, sort of. We didn't have sex, I've never had sex, we just made out all night and I touched his dick. Not very much, though. I think dicks are kind of gross.

We went back to the dorms at around two in the morning and then I left with my parents at nine this morning to drive back home. Glen was cute, I guess. He didn't have a nasty body like most wrestlers. He was pretty boring, though. I remember asking him questions about Las Vegas and him giving me shitty answers. Awkward silences ensued, and then I'd drunkenly ask the same questions over again, forgetting that he'd already answered. So we made out, instead.

This weekend I'm going to be visiting the school in Seattle that I've been looking at most seriously. I hope it compares with the school in Portland because the Seattle soccer team is way better.

23 April 2008

Today was all right until Calculus. Two hours of hatred and confusion tampers with my mindset. It put me in a horrible mood, and from then on everything that was slightly annoying made me quite agitated. I had soccer, though, and it was good and now I feel better.

Davis sent me this note during fourth period inviting me to go mini-golfing with him during prom weekend, but not go to prom since we both think it's stupid. I met him in Newspaper last year, and he's in that class again this year. In Newspaper you can call students out of other classes to interview them, so sometimes he calls me out of boring classes or sends notes to me.

Anyway, I don't want to go because I decided I don't like him like that. He is too nerdy and gangly and always telling me boring stories. I am not attracted to him at all anymore! I don't even know why I was. I think because he is smart and in Newspaper he was always concentrating really hard on whatever he was doing and I liked distracting him with my feminine energy.

24 April 2008

I watched *Adaptation*, and it was one of the most fucked up movies I've ever seen. It was strange. And it had scenes from *Being John Malkovich*, which was weird because I just saw that movie! It was so incredibly strange. It was a movie that described exactly the way I talk to myself in my head.

27 April 2008

The past couple of days I was in Seattle, and I fell in love with the city. It's huge, with tons of artsy shops and stores, a big market by the water with every kind of food imaginable, and skyscrapers, all overcast gray. It's close to the university as well, which has a gorgeous campus. Everything is green and lush.

I visited "The Jungle" where the senior soccer girls live, and it is probably the coolest house I've ever been to. It's covered in vines and flowers and has a little backyard with grass. There are three floors: a downstairs, middle floor, and an upstairs. There are two kitchens and this sweet hangout place downstairs. All the girls were nice and they introduced themselves and answered all my questions.

I hung out with one of the sophomores on the soccer team and her friends. We ate at this bubble tea shop in the University District. Bubble tea is sort of like a smoothie or a milkshake, depending on what flavor you get. They put tapioca balls at the bottom, which is kind of weird to me. Later we went to a laser show where you lay on the ground in the dark and they play a whole album of music really loud (they played Radiohead for us) and put laser designs all over the ceiling.

We also went to the Seattle Center and there was this hippie festival going on with tons of weird, creative people with dreads and grungy fashion. Everyone was making and selling art and jewelry, and playing music with strange instruments, and smoking mota. Culture! There is much more culture there than in Boise, I love it.

The university is a private, religious school so I was afraid that no one would drink or smoke because I'm pretty sure they prohibit that kind of stuff on campus. But this girl on the team said that you can always find people that want to do the things you want to do. She said she knows people that get drunk all the time, so I was reassured.

Not that I only want to get drunk all the time, but people that do those things are more open-minded I feel like. Also, Sawyer is always telling me about crazy college parties he's attended and it sounds exciting. I'm also not religious at all; in fact, I am exceedingly un-religious, so I am unsure what the vibe will be like.

And...I'm committing tomorrow! I talked to my club soccer coach about it, and I'm going to call the Seattle coach tomorrow and tell him that I'd like to commit to them. I am extremely happy to be done with all this stuff, like emailing and calling coaches...It's just overwhelming!

28 April 2008

Books are people, and reading them is meeting people. And it's amazing because I don't have to talk to them; I just listen, and it's not boring. It's not like someone is rambling on and on. It's interesting, and I have power over them in such a way that I can stop them from talking whenever I want, and tell them to begin again in exactly the same place, without them losing their train of thought. It's a beautiful analogy.

30 April 2008

I'm in a bad mood for several reasons. Here is a list:

• I don't want to go mini-golfing with Davis.

• I have been doing badly at soccer and my ankle hurts.

• I have to call some lady for my job-shadow project for English and talking on the phone makes me extremely anxious, especially when it has something to do with more than a simple doctor's appointment.

• I have to email my English teacher in two days about my job-shadow progress, and we never even got a rubric for the job-shadow.

• My life is consumed by school and could be consumed by work when I'm older, which makes life seem so boring and pointless.

• I have to take the SAT on Saturday.

• I don't understand Calculus at all.

• We have a different schedule at school tomorrow which is shittiness. I hate when they change the schedule!

• I never (hardly ever) talk to Eli and he's my best friend.

• I ate too much before soccer practice and I felt shitty.

• I'm in love with Zack de la Rocha, the Rage Against the

Machine lead singer, and I'm afraid I'll never meet anyone like him.

• I don't want to become older.

• There are so many pointless rules that don't help anything or anyone at school.

• I have a $20 fine for a lost book at the school library, and the librarians lost it.

• I want to kill every character in The Crucible, which is what we are reading in English, except John Proctor, and anyone else like that in the world that can be extraordinarily FUCKING STUPID!

Well, that's all folks! I'm sure I could find a few other things that are pissing me off, but I already feel a tad better so I'll just stop.

01 May 2008

I am on my period, that could be why I felt terrible yesterday. I feel better today.

Davis figured out where I park my car and he parked there today, which is fucking stalkerish!

I called this lady at Edward's Greenhouse about job-shadowing, because I feel like it'd be cool to work in a greenhouse, and she said she'd call me back in the next few days because she didn't know if they have it or not. So that's kind of inconvenient, but whatever.

04 May 2008

Yesterday I took the SAT and I think I did well. And then

Davis picked me up and we went mini-golfing. It was actually sort of fun, I didn't think it was going to be. I thought he was gonna make a move on me or something; that's why I was dreading it. But he didn't, so everything was good.

05 May 2008

Yesterday Eli and I went on a bike ride on the greenbelt, and we made peanut butter and honey sandwiches, and had a picnic, and made hemp stuff at the park by the river. It was so much fun! On the way home we walked out on this log in the water and decided to go for a swim, so we stripped down to our underwear and jumped in the freezing water. It was very James Bondish. Actually, it was more like teenage-runaway-do-whatever-we-feel-like-ish. Which is awesome.

12 May 2008

Today I woke at eight and went to the elementary school Mom works at around nine to do my job-shadow with this lady that teaches technology classes, or classes that use newer technologies, or something. Since Mom works there it was really easy to set up, and the lady at Edward's Greenhouse never called me back, so…yeah.

I talked with the tech lady and watched her two classes. It wasn't bad at all. She showed me a few other classes and introduced me to some of the teachers. I ate a donut in the teachers' lounge, heated up. I read my book for a while and then I went home, ate a muffin, and now I'm at the public library. I rode my bike over here and I'm going to work on some stuff.

16 May 2008

Yesterday we got up early and drove to LA for Sawyer's graduation ceremony. It was such a long drive, and the ceremony today was long, too. The speeches before the separate majors had their own walks were super boring, so I texted Camila and we quoted *Zoolander* to each other for, like, two hours. Sawyer's walk was in the building where they hold the Academy Awards, and it was pretty cool, but also boring because there were a lot of people to walk and it took forever.

This morning before the ceremony I ate a croissant and coffee for breakfast real early and then ate nothing until about two p.m. I felt like I was going to faint. Our family and one of Sawyer's friends drove to In-N-Out Burger to eat, and I closed my eyes the whole way because I had no energy. The drive was long, too, since there is always a lot of traffic in LA. After that we drove back to Sawyer's place, and only Mom and Dad and I went back to our hotel in Long Beach and went shopping.

We went to Buffalo Exchange and I got this sweet belt. Everything there was more expensive than usual, which was annoying. I guess that's what happens when you're in a big city.

I was super out of it because I was so tired, so when this college guy at a shoe store tried to have a conversation with me, I was like, "Go away!" Not really, just in my head. I was exhausted and I couldn't even think about talking to someone, much less form coherent sentences. But I think he thought I was in college, because when I told him I was a junior in high school he just kind of walked away awkwardly. Haha. It was hilarious. I think he was hitting on me and felt dumb when he realized I'm in high school.

We went to dinner at this expensive restaurant because a lot of Sawyer's friends on the swim team were going there with their families. We spent about $200 on food. Yikes.

Tomorrow we are going to say bye to Sawyer. He's going to Texas with a friend, and then heading to Reno to visit my grandpa before going back to Boise.

28 May 2008

Today I was frustrated and unhappy. I'm on my period so that could be a major cause of my discontent. Calculus was a big factor: I'm doing a project with this girl named Sarah. She's just an acquaintance. She did the calculations wrong I'm sure, but I feel like I can't tell her that because I'm not the math genius. I feel like a lot of the time I'm stupid. I feel like I'm less intelligent than her and everyone else in my classes.

Sarah told me that according to her life plan she should be writing her first novel this summer. And I thought that was kind of stupid. Who writes out when they are going to write their first novel? Wouldn't they just do it?*

[*Ana: People that are on top of their shit and that know what they want do this. It's good to create goals and write them down because you're far more likely to follow through with them if you write them down first. You don't know what you want yet. She does. –J.]

And I think (I don't know, of course) that she feels intellectually superior to me. And that makes me feel like shit, especially when I love writing and reading and she decides that she is so fantastic at both that she should be done with her first novel by this summer.

I don't know. I guess I just feel threatened by her. I feel like a lot of people think I'm stupid. I dunno, maybe they have a right to since I do talk often of my loathing of Calculus and my inability to get good grades in it.

And today, my club soccer coach was telling my team that college soccer is going to be super hard and that we need to be really committed, and I felt like I suck at soccer and that when I get to college they are all going to be so much better than me. I only feel this way because I haven't been juggling a ball on my own time. But I will. Tomorrow I'll at least juggle. But for now I need to sleep.

Tomorrow is probably going to be another shitty day where I worry about stupid bullshit and have to do a fuckton of work that I don't want to do.

29 May 2008

Today I lost my school ID and driver's license during lunch. When they called me down to the office to pick them up, because someone found them and turned them in, the stupid attendance guy interrogated me about my teacher not checking my ID, and gave me a lecture about how she should have.

He said, "So who should I give lunch detention to, you or Mrs. Wayne?" I was like, "YOU ARE SO FUCKING STUPID!" I didn't really say that, obviously. He ended up not giving me lunch detention, so that was cool. Not that I'd go anyway…God, I hate how they treat us like idiots here!

Also, I might start the Calculus final tomorrow, and I didn't study at all. Well, I tried to, sort of. I just didn't know where to start, or what to study, or where everything was in my notes. So ultimately, I'm going to fail it. But I do not care because I FUCKING HATE CALCULUS SO MUCH! It is the source of all my confusion and depression and self-loathing and frustrated melancholy.

01 June 2008

We drove to Lewiston with Grandma this past weekend to take her home. She was staying with us for a couple weeks. I slept almost the whole way so the trip seemed very short. I listened to Mirah. I like her song called "La familia." When we got to Lewiston we went to Grandma's first, then to Camila's work to say hi. Later that night Camila and I went to this kid Kevin's house and played drinking games with him and some other people.

I feel like Camila's friends are much more creative and artistic and nicer than anyone at my school. I like hanging out with them and doing things that people in high school are supposed to experiment with. They are like "indie kids" if I had to stereotype them. I think maybe I like that vibe a lot and would like to be one of them if I could pick a stereotype for myself. I don't think I'm easily stereotyped, though.

Kevin kissed me, kind of; like a peck on the lips when we were leaving. It was weird. Camila and I got home at midnight and played Nintendo and snacked a ton because we had the drunk munchies, and then went to bed. I woke up early today, had some breakfast, and Mom and I left for home.

05 June 2008

All right! Today is the first day of summer. I took my Calculus and science finals, and I guessed on literally everything on my Calculus final. I checked my grade today and I got an 80%! What the fuck!? I don't know how that

43

happened. Apparently I am an amazing guesser and God exists. Or maybe my teacher felt bad for me and lied in the gradebook. Haha. But I got an 87% in the class, which is fucking incredible.

Last night Jenna and I slept in her tent in her backyard. We watched *The Thief Lord* and made a chocolate cake. It was delish. We had it for a midnight snack as well as breakfast. Yes!

10 June 2008

I've been thinking about a lot of things. It seems like lately I've had trouble extracting pure thought from my mind. When I got up this morning after strange and vivid dreams, everything looked foreign to me. The butter in its circular plastic container, how bright the sun was, my legs, the way our bodies are shaped, my senses.

The way I see the leaves on the neighbors' trees so far up, pulsating in the wind, shiny and reflecting white light from the sun. It looks like the limbs are coming alive and fighting each other. The leaves are vicious, snapping creatures.

Cars and the way the wheels turn, books, the concept of books. Me. My brain is made of chemicals and energy and fuels my body through hormonal mechanisms. I am entirely made of energy. I can't control the way I think. What do I think? Why do I think? What is thought? Energy. I realized how good it feels to lay on something warm. How simple pleasures are overlooked, unnoticed. Warmth, food, senses.

13 June 2008

Circles. Catch 22's. Nothing matters! I can think and feel and sense, but what for?

I watched *Steel Toes* with Eli last night. It's a movie about a skinhead that kicked this guy basically to death. He later died in the hospital. The skinhead eventually realized how utterly sickening his crime was. The guy on the ground pleaded with him but he still kicked him as hard as he could and wouldn't stop.

When the skinhead remembered this and later read a letter of forgiveness from the man he kicked, he threw up everywhere because he realized how disgusting that was to be able to do that to a human being. He cried and screamed and coughed and vomited.

I keep wondering, how could a person do that? How could a person be so brutally filled with hatred and anger? These bubble to the surface and easily show their face. Humans become animals. Dignity washes away like drawings in the sand taken by the ocean.

I feel like a person has to use a lot more brainpower to feel that strongly, on either side: attacker or victim. After a person has gone through such an enlightening experience, an experience that truly changes who she is, who she will be, who she would have been, I think her brain has been stretched to its ultimate limits of sensory function. She probably feels so much more strongly than others in moments like this. It's incredible to me.

I want to feel more than I can but I can't simulate any situations that would make me feel more. I was on the brink of something real when watching *Steel Toes*, but I couldn't grasp it. The visual and auditory examples went by way too quickly. I think the throwing up was the key.

14 June 2008

Can unity and individualism be combined?

15 June 2008

Right now I'm reading the book *Fight Club*, which is crazy good. I like it a lot because it makes me feel a bit scared and uncomfortable, but excited and almost liberated as well. I'd like to be a part of some huge secret like that, hidden in barroom basements after hours and smeared with someone else's blood.

20 June 2008

Yesterday I played in an indoor soccer game and I rolled my right ankle and it popped, and now my foot is swollen and I can barely walk on it. I'm icing and elevating right now, and I'm scared that I won't be able to play in U.S. Club Regionals. I don't understand why bad things like this always happen to me. I'm angry and sad and frustrated.

I don't have practice for four more days though, so that's good. I just hope that this was for a reason, like maybe something really bad won't happen to me now because I won't be in that situation since I can't walk. If I hadn't hurt it I would have been in the situation and something worse would have happened. I like to think of it that way.

I finished reading a book about Buddhism while icing my ankle. It fucked with my mind. Buddhism is intense and contradictory, but in a good way. A lot of it I can connect with and think is true about the universe, like about balance and clearing one's mind.

But then there are parts that only confuse me because they seem contradictory, and still more parts that I'm kind of skeptical about. But it's all very interesting and I'd like to research it a lot more. I feel like it's the most objective thing I have ever experienced regarding spirituality.

23 June 2008

I should remember that nothing ever matters, these people don't matter, the world is an illusion. Which reminds me of the ongoing interest I have in Buddhism. It kind of fucks with my mind, though. It makes statements about becoming enlightened, and I feel like I would have no interests or anything if I did become enlightened. And that sounds boring and bad, but then I think that if I were enlightened, it wouldn't be boring or bad to me.

I want to experience different aspects of the world though, in ways that Buddhists wouldn't, and in ways that they would. I think I should do what I want and have fun and do the things that make me happy. Sometimes I think it's good to succumb to desires, even though I don't think Buddhists think that's good. I don't know, I feel like sometimes they do. It's all very confusing because I find so many contradictions.

25 June 2008

I went to soccer yesterday and today, and my ankle was fine. I'm pretty relieved! Yesterday I wore a brace but it was hurting the bottom of my foot so I didn't wear it today. Tomorrow practice is cancelled because our coach is "tired and burnt out." Tomorrow I have another indoor game at 11 p.m. I hope my ankle doesn't get fucked up. I'll wear cleats and go easy on it.

Right now I'm going to watch a movie and ice my ankle. I don't feel like watching *House of 1000 Corpses* or *South Park*, which is all I have at home right now, so I dunno what I'll do.

30 June 2008

Right now I'm watching *House of 1000 Corpses* and it is so fucked up I can't even explain it to you. I went to practice this morning but this girl Toree on my team kicked my ankle and it popped, so I sat out for the rest of it and iced. Our coach gave me money to go buy ice at the gas station by the field. He told me to go into his car and get money out of his wallet, and I felt really uncomfortable doing that.

03 July 2008

Today I went to soccer and it was frustrating. I feel slow and I have an awful touch right now. It's really bothering me. I just did some yoga, but I couldn't stop thinking and worrying about all the shit I have to do and about soccer and about my stupid rubberbands for my braces. And I am always on the go or getting something done and I need to learn to slow it down.

I dunno, maybe I was expecting some miraculous peace of mind free from all anxieties after doing my yoga, and it didn't come. And I feel super anxious right now.

04 July 2008

Last night Jenna and I slept outside on the trampoline in her backyard, but the sprinklers came on at four in the morning so we got all wet and startled and went inside.

She was annoying me because she was talking about God to

me before we fell asleep, and I didn't say anything because I knew if I did I would just blurt out about how God doesn't exist and how I don't care at all, and that would only start a pointless fight which would irritate me even more.

I'm sick of hearing bullshit about God; at least the Christian, white, father-figure God. God is something humans made up to explain our existence because we can't accept the mystery of life.* We can't accept that we have no fucking clue about who and what we are. We can't accept that we feel so alone.

[*Ana: Research astrology and other occult subjects. Research Carl Jung. Nature is God. Everything is energy. Everything is connected. –J.]

We can't accept that the only person one can completely and absolutely trust is herself. And even that is dubious only because we are human (a term that in itself is questionable) and we make mistakes. Without a god we start to doubt ourselves, because we couldn't trust ourselves in the first place.

The world is a terrifying, lonely abyss. We need order and routine, someone to tell us what to do. To me, the concept of God is generally completely irrelevant in my life. I don't need God because all I need is emptiness. I know what's in my subconscious. Thoughts bubble to the surface and I gather them and clear them away with a pen and paper. What I try to do is question my assumptions. Think creatively, you know?

17 July 2008

Today life was surreal. Björk and Smashing Pumpkins haunted me all day with beautiful music that makes me feel so indescribable, and I was everywhere and nowhere. Everything mattered, but nothing did. I felt free because I truly didn't care about anything. I did things because I wanted to and I am 17 years old and I'm a free spirit.

I love art and fashion and music and life. I breathed in deep lungfuls of air, and I waved my hair around and sensed the sun and the wind, and my head was turning around and around and I could see everything. My body trapped me in, held me back from all there is to experience, and I was so sad. But at the same time it was beautiful emotion.

I long to be able to fly and twirl and I hate that my mind does these things to me. I want to be Björk because she's genuine and complex and different, and her musical expression has impacted my perspective on everything. I long for freaky outfits and multi-colored hair.

23 July 2008

Last night I slept over at Kourtney's house with three other girls and some of their guy friends. Kourtney and the other girls are on my club soccer team and invited me to their little party. We drank beer and played beer pong and smoked weed and Prime Times. It was fun, I guess. I didn't get that drunk or anything. I didn't throw up.

I don't really like those people. I mean, I guess I like the girls on my team, I just can't connect with them. I don't really care about what they care about. They're just average people like everybody else. They're not that real. And those guys were stupid and exactly like the stereotypical assholes I hate at school.

24 July 2008

I watch a lot of movies and I read a lot of books because

honestly, real life is boring. I wish I could have a real adventure, with danger and exotic places and interesting people and situations, where I'd have to be cunning and smart and athletic and witty, but it's like nothing ever happens like that. I wish something magical would happen. I wish there were monsters and faeries and strange things that don't make any sense.

At the same time, I read about people that live in a world just like ours, with no magic or anything, just normal people, and the way they think and act and are described enthralls me. What they do is fantastic to me, and when I look at my life I want to see myself as if I were the protagonist in a well-written novel. I want to look at my life through curious and awed eyes. I want to be exquisite and mysterious.

WHY? WHY ANYTHING? I write papers for school so I can get a good grade, so I can go to college and get a good job that pays a lot so I can eat good food and sleep in and buy things that make me happy. But why? We live in a material world but none of it seems to matter.

What matters is the mind and the feelings, and the way you look up from your book when you're riding the bus to meet the gaze of a stranger and wonder what she's thinking. The way the sun feels on your skin and how that compares to the way you feel inside when you see someone you love and it makes you smile.

Is there a way other than chemicals and neurons in the brain? Is there an existence contrary to ours? Something living unlike us? Another dimension? Something that cannot be perceived in the way we perceive?

30 July 2008

I knew I wouldn't write over the weekend…I went to Virginia for U.S. Club Regionals!

We had three layovers on the way to Virginia. One was three hours long. I rode first class twice on the way there, it was sweet. I roomed with three girls on my team, and the hotel was nasty. Everything was damp and gross and it was just sick.

In our first game we played this team from New Jersey, I think, and they weren't even good, but they scored three goals on us! It was fucked up. The refs and our luck were terrible, it was disappointing.

In our second game I scored and then our goalie fucked us by obviously fouling this girl after she caught the ball, giving them a free kick, which they scored on. And then they scored this other stupid goal that I didn't even see, but oh my god it was ridiculous. So we were automatically out of the championship. We won our third game, though.

On our down time we went to the beach and swam way far out. We also swam in the hotel pool. We went out to dinner a few times. Yesterday we had a whole day to spend doing whatever, so we watched our younger team in the championship game, which they lost. It was miserable: hot, humid, sweaty, sticky. But we did get to eat donuts and orange juice on the sideline.

We went to the beach again after and shopped in all these stores, and I bought a blue shirt that says Virginia Beach under a white peace sign. I stole Kourtney a silver ring and myself a blue bracelet with a silver peace sign. Then we ate at some random restaurant. We also changed hotels to a much better one by the airport.

Today we had to get up at 3:45 a.m. to leave for the airport.

Miserable. Right now I'm on the second flight, to Phoenix, and I slept for a long time. Now I'm listening to Gorillaz and writing. I have to pee very badly but I'm trapped by the window. I guess I'll just have to ask to get out. I hate doing that.

01 August 2008

I've felt detached from society a lot lately. I asked Dad if he believes in God and he said no. I don't think I do either anymore. Now I kind of think it's stupid to believe in God. It's weird because almost everyone, okay, maybe not almost everyone, just a lot of people, are religious and I think it's bullshit. I mean, I do think the concept of religion and the content of different religions are interesting to learn about, but I don't know if I believe any of it. I don't think I do. I think I believe Buddhists, because they have no God.

I'm trying to be more bad, because you only live one lifetime, and I want to do whatever the fuck I want because it's my life, and my life isn't fucked up in any way, I don't think. I mean, I don't have serious issues or problems like a lot of people. I just want to live. So I want to try shrooms and do other drugs just to try them.*

They kind of scare me though, because I'm afraid I'll kill someone or something while on them, and not know what I'm doing. That not only scares me because I would be in deep shit, but also because I don't like the idea of not being in control of my mind and body. In a way I want to try these things to assure myself that I can handle it. That I'm in control. And also normal human curiosity, I guess.

[*Ana: Just stay the fuck away from opioids and meth. Hallucinogens will inevitably teach you something interesting and

53

most likely spiritual or metaphysical. Remember, everything in moderation (even moderation). Except for opioids and meth. Stay the FUCK away from opioids and meth! Also, alcohol is bad for you too. Way worse for you than mota. –J.]

02 August 2008

Today some of my family from Dad's side came over and we visited all day and barbecued. I read the first part of *Crime and Punishment* for my future English class (we have homework even though it's summer and we won't meet until school starts again) and I wrote a summary of that part, which I will have to turn in eventually. I felt pretty awkward around everyone.

I felt scared of myself. In *Crime and Punishment* the protagonist is like me. And he ends up bashing this old lady's head in with an ax. I'm scared of myself because sometimes when I see a knife I imagine plunging it into whoever is with me at the time. I imagine the cry escaping one's mouth, born of confusion and surprise, the look on a person's face during a terrible death, and I'm horrified. I think about how easy it would be to kill someone.

Sometimes, when I'm driving home late at night, I imagine driving off the road into a building or something at high speed. How easy it would be to end all the meaningless suffering. All you have to do is turn the wheel.

I'm tortured by the fact that I'm human. I don't know what anything is anymore. I don't know what I am. I don't know if what is real is all that is real. I don't know what real is. I feel like no one could ever understand me, or this: what I'm writing. I'm just really confused right now.

04 August 2008

Yesterday I went to Lisbet's, and we smoked a lot and watched *The Holiday* and ate pizza. Then Alyssa hung out with us for a while, but she had to be home by midnight. Lisbet's mom bought us alcohol. It was fun. I slept over at her house and we went to bed at, like, three in the morning. This morning she had work at 11 so we got up around ten and I left shortly thereafter. I went on a run when I got back, which was hell, but I felt good after it.

06 August 2008

I'm so tired. I watched *Nova ScienceNow* with my parents, and it made me realize how much there is to know in the world, in the universe, in life, in everything. It was just extremely overwhelming and frustrating and I cried because I felt worried and stupid for feeling worried. I felt really terrible for a while.

09 August 2008

My parents have been annoying the fuck out of me lately.

10 August 2008

This is the beginning of the end. End of a diary, end of summer. Tomorrow I register for my last year in high school. I have soccer tryouts, and I'll see Eli!

11 August 2008

Last night I hung out with Lisbet, and all we did was drive around in her car and smoke mota. Eventually we went to her sister's house downtown and watched the Olympics on her tiny TV and ate the vegan food she made us. We also walked to this ice cream place right by her house.

When we got back to her house we smoked out of this gravity bong her sister made, and all I took was one giant hit, and I got so incredibly high. I didn't feel well at all. I felt instant nausea, and my head ached and I could barely walk. My throat burned. Basically, it was a terrible experience. When we got back to Lisbet's house I vomited in her toilet downstairs. I was kind of glad to throw up because I ate a lot of food when I wasn't really hungry, and I felt much better afterwards.

It was scary because I had to talk to Dad on the phone amidst the post gravity bong events to tell him that I was going to stay at Lisbet's house that night (too fucked up to drive home), and I was terrified that I'd say something weird or wouldn't be able to concentrate. But it ended up being okay.

This morning I had to wake up at six to get my stuff at home so I could go to soccer tryouts for high school, which were a joke. High school soccer is the worst, but during the fall that's what I have to do. Club soccer is way better and more competitive.

In between tryouts Lisbet and I registered for school and went to Eli's house and swam in his pool with him and his best friend Tyler who also plays soccer and is on Eli's club team. He'll probably be on the varsity team at school this year as well. He was on it last year so that would make sense. He plays center back and runs kind of funny with his arms at weird angles. We all went to the second tryout session together, which was hot and frustrating and not fun at all.

Jenna and I hung out today. I felt comfortable with her.

Usually I get annoyed with her really fast, especially when she starts talking about Jesus, but I didn't today. A lot of the time I think the things she does are kind of dumb or something, but today I thought everything was cool.

It's hard to explain, but it's like there are some people that I think do and have super interesting things automatically. I guess it's kind of biased. Like, for example, Lisbet's sister I think is cool automatically. I don't even try to think for myself and have opinions different from hers when I'm around her. I think everything she does is great for some reason I'm unaware of.

Around Jenna, it's exactly the opposite. I seem to be negative around her and I disagree with a lot of what she says. Both situations I don't like. So I'm not going to think everything Lisbet's sister does is cool (and I don't think it's just her that I feel that way about; she's just an example) and I'm not going to think that everything Jenna does is dumb. At least I'm going to try not to think that.

14 August 2008

Yesterday I watched a movie called *The Edukators*, and it is a brilliant film. It's in German, so all English subtitles for me. It's about these three people that break into rich people's homes and rearrange all their furniture, but don't steal anything, and then leave menacing notes commenting on how the people have too much money. I thought it was beautiful, genius, an excellent idea. It would be such a rush to do that.

Why are there no adventures here? This is all I want. Something exciting and revolutionary and fueled by thought.

18 August 2008

I'm reading *Breaking Dawn* and it makes me depressed. There are vampires in this book (I know, it's ridiculous. I just wanted to see why everyone is obsessed with it) and they don't have to rely on sleeping, and they live forever. I wish I didn't have to rely on sleeping and eating and going to the bathroom. I want to live forever because there is an impossible amount of things to do, things to learn and see and feel and experience. So many books to read, so many people to know.

I also watched *The Time Machine* today, and it made me feel dumbfounded because time stretches on for infinity. There are too many places to explore, especially in the years to come. In the millions of years to come the world will be an entirely different place.

I'm so goddamn curious about all the things! I figure I only have about 100 years to do everything I want until I die. Not enough time. Maybe I'll be reincarnated and get to live another lifetime of experiences. Maybe I've already lived a billion lifetimes. Everything is just too crazy to think about.

20 August 2008

Lisbet and I got high before the high school soccer retreat yesterday. We both made the varsity team again; no surprise there. It was fun. We kept saying "I don't give a fuck!" We kept saying that over and over in different voices, it was hilarious. Then at the retreat we played random games and watched *Coach Carter*. I fell asleep during it because I don't like sports movies.

Then this morning at six we went on a run. It felt good to run in the cold and see the morning clouds before the sun rose. It felt good to push my muscles, to stretch them and inhale the darkness. I really love the darkness. The way it embraces and holds me, the way no one can see me, the way it makes all my movements stealthy. The fear it brings. The coldness of it on my skin. It makes me feel alive.

21 August 2008

I hung out with Lisbet and Conrad today, and then we picked up two of Conrad's friends and smoked mota by the river. Conrad goes to our school and I had a huge crush on him freshman year. He has straight, dirty blonde hair that is shaggy and sort of long, and he is a genius at math, which I think is super sexy.

After that, Lisbet and I went to the grocery store to buy food. We saw these kids from school that she knows, and as much as I didn't want to, we went to their house and smoked in their garage. I left as soon as I could. I wasn't in that great of a mood and we were doing things that I had no patience for.

This stupid kid was talking about how dumb the "scene" kids are, and that really annoyed me how he was categorizing people and being judgmental. It's okay to categorize people if you are trying to describe them, but to say that all the people in that category are stupid…*that's* stupid.

The garage we smoked in was hotter than hell, and I had a terrible time. I don't want to smoke as much as I have been, which isn't even that much, but still. To tell you the truth, I don't even like it that much. It's cool to do just because it's illegal, but I actually like being in my right mind and knowing what's going on around me.

I do like resisting authority, but smoking mota is kind of nasty. It's annoying because you can't be serious or have a real, intelligent conversation with someone.* I never get that high, so it's like I'm all alone because I'm almost normal and everyone else is like, "haha, what?" And when I do get high I just get anxious and paranoid and scared. Or I throw up. It sucks.

[*Ana: Yes, you can have a real conversation with people after smoking. You're doing it with the wrong people. You're also doing it wrong in general. You should try doing it alone and going on a long walk. –J.]

22 August 2008

Davis wanted to go to the fair with me, so I invited Lisbet because I didn't want to be alone with him because it would be awkward. We eventually didn't go because Lisbet wanted to get mota and it took her forever and we didn't have enough time after that. I was glad, though, because I didn't have to spend money to get into the fair.

Later we smoked with Conrad at his house and I got higher than I have been in a long time, which was cool, I guess. Conrad is a genius. He's nerdy like Davis except cuter and a huge pot-head. If he weren't high at every moment in his life I would be in love with him.

Right now I'm reading a book called *The Acid House* by Irvine Welsh, who also wrote *Trainspotting*, which I didn't read but I saw the movie and it's super good. It's hard to read though, because he writes weirdly a lot of the time in order to reflect a specific dialect of English. I like the chapters "Euro-trash" and "A Smart Cunt."

Sometimes all I can think is why is he writing about me? I think he gets it. It seriously freaks me out how much he gets it. I feel so anxious all the time and his explanations of his characters' feelings could probably explain why.

24 August 2008

Today is the last day of summer. Tomorrow is the first day of school and the worst day of my life. Right now it is 11:42 p.m. and I'm about to go to bed. Goodbye summer. Goodbye freedom.

25 August 2008

Today was the first day of school and it wasn't too bad; I'm still alive at least. Eli is not in any of my classes. Neither is Lisbet. But Jessi is in my psychology class, which is cool. She's on the varsity soccer team and plays defense. She is kind of thick-set. We aren't super good friends or anything, but at least I'll have someone I know in class so it won't be scary.

I didn't get into Spanish because I could only take it if I dropped Advanced Placement English, and there's no way I'm doing that. Not after reading *Crime and Punishment*! But, I suppose I wouldn't have traded it anyway.

26 August 2008

Today in Government I felt stupid because I forgot to write the paragraph that was our homework. So I wrote, like, three sentences while my classmates were turning theirs in, and everyone else's were like half a page long. It gave me a lot of anxiety.

And also, I know nothing about government and I really don't want her to call on me in class when I'm not wanting to be called on (which is always). Which means that I will probably get called on a lot and be humiliated in front of everybody, like, every day. Yes! Just what I wanted!

Also, today in English I felt stupid because I felt like my *Crime and Punishment* journals sucked because I wasn't one of the people our professor picked to read hers out loud, even though those were like five people out of the whole class. So that was dumb of me to get depressed over.

But also, I don't think Raskolnikov, the main character, is crazy, and everyone else does. I know that I should think my own things and be different, but I feel super self-conscious and stupid at school.

I feel like I'm going insane sometimes. I feel like killing myself. I think about it at least once a day. But I know I'm above suicide. And I want to live. I'm smart enough to control myself when I get overwhelmed. I'm smart enough to not let people know what I'm thinking and feeling. I'm smart enough to work the system.

What my problem is, is that I know who and what I am, but I'm not satisfied. I hate school and the people irritate me. Maybe I have no fucking clue about who I am. This is the problem: I don't know which is true. I don't know anything.

I always think about famous writers and artists that killed themselves or had depression, or went through failure many times and had hardships that were real. Not like me just feeling self-conscious at school. I want to be one of these people. I don't know if I'm trying to be like them and that's why I feel so down and depressed a lot because I'm forcing it on myself, or if it's actually real and true.

I want to be one of these superhumans that Raskolnikov wanted to be, someone above the law and other people. Maybe that's not really who I want to be though, because these artists and writers I look up to feel (or felt) depression and sadness and other things that supposedly superhumans wouldn't.

Maybe I'm the lowest of the low and everybody else is above me. And maybe I haven't really failed at anything...

27 August 2008

Who are we to determine who is crazy? Who is mentally ill? We are nothing. We don't matter. We feel these things for no reason, and if someone feels differently, is it our right to classify him as mentally ill? So what if a person murders someone else? Doesn't matter. Nothing happens. There is no afterlife. There is no god. If he feels guilty, if he has remorse, it's his own dilemma. If someone then murders him in revenge, he'd have to know he had it coming. And would we call that person crazy? Not crazy, no. Aware of his feelings. A difference in emotion, perhaps. A unique mind structure.

28 August 2008

I feel better now, but today was pretty weird. At school we had an assembly at lunch, so it took up a lot of time and I only had 20 minutes to eat when it was over. I really didn't want to go, but River, my tall and fashionable male friend, told me, "You're gonna get caught when you try to leave!" So I was like, "Ugh, I'll just go," and I don't know why I did that. I don't know why I didn't just leave, it would have been so simple. I could have started running as soon as I got out the doors.

I didn't want to attend the assembly because it would take forever and I wouldn't be able to go to anyone's house to eat, and I didn't bring money or a lunch so I'd be starving, and I had fitness class after. Assemblies are fucking stupid. They are boring as fuck and we do school pride bullshit and I start to hate everybody, more than I already do, and it's cramped and hot and stuffy. I found Eli, though, and sat by him.

I was in the worst mood because I thought about all the things I could have been doing instead of that bullshit, and I was pissed because I only have so long to live before I die and this was wasting my time.

Eli said, "You look like you're in so much pain right now," and I don't even know if I was just making all these feelings up or if I actually felt them, and that made me mad and I felt dumb. All of this could be PMS or something, because I think I'm supposed to be starting my period soon, but I haven't yet.

Then, when the assembly was finally over, I just wanted out of there, and I couldn't breathe because there were a ton of people crowding me and pushing, and I felt like I was going to start crying because it was so bad. I went to my car and sat there and called Lisbet, but she'd already left. I saw Eli and Tyler leaving, so I called them, but I decided I wouldn't have time to go with them. When I was talking to Eli on the phone I started crying, so I hung up.

I don't know what's wrong with me. Lisbet ended up buying me breadsticks for lunch so I got to eat. After school I went home and took a nap before soccer. When I woke up I was really scared. Of myself. It was actually quite frightening for about five minutes. I was just consumed with fear of what I'm capable of.

Like, sometimes I'm afraid that I'm going to snap one day and try to kill myself. I don't think it'll happen, but it's always a possibility. That's what scary: there's always a possibility! I could do too many terrible things. And why don't I?

What's in my mind that holds me back from ripping people apart? Knowledge of consequences? I have to hold myself together and one thing that I do it for is knowing that I'm going to college and I can't fuck that up. That's why I try to do well in school even when I want to kill everyone.

I seriously don't know if I'm truly feeling all this shit! Or if I'm trying to be all dark and depressed or something, or just pretending. Which is fucked up. I feel like I'm not real. Maybe I take everything way too seriously and overreact. Lately, I've been thinking about people's minds, and psychology, and how easily we can be manipulated, and I don't give a fuck what people think. Not that I ever did, anyway; it's just heightened lately, maybe?

I think that people are only beings that think and feel according to chemical reactions responding to outside forces. Which makes me think about how nothing matters and why do we do things? Why does anyone do anything? Existence is overbearing and overwhelming. I'm here, and I don't know what to do with myself.

What are we, why are we here? There are no answers and I can't handle that. I don't even know what I'm talking about anymore.

Sometimes I want to scream at people, "You don't know anything about anything! Shut up! There is so much more to life than all your stupid bullshit about your boyfriends and your drama and your body and your makeup!" It takes a lot to hold it in.

29 August 2008

Yesterday I went to Lisbet's, and we hung out and I slept over. We smoked, and I sent a picture of the mota to Davis because it was a huge nugget or bud or whatever you call it. He started lecturing me about how smoking can't be good for my soccer. He mentioned that the last time I did it was only three days ago, when it was actually, like, eight days ago. It really irritated me!

He acted like my mother or something. Or my boyfriend. Which he will never be. It kind of grossed me out. We have no classes together, thank god. He's nice and stuff, but we have nothing in common and he usually tells me boring stories about nothing in particular and we don't talk about anything serious.

Oh, and I have to go to ice cream with him, and I don't want to! He texted me and told me about all this music shit, and about people that are going to play here, and I was like, "Oh my god, shut up! I do not care!" In my head, of course. Then he said, "I have a coupon for ice cream that expires soon…" Which was the beginning of hell for me.

I made so many fucking excuses until I had no more, and he still didn't get the hint.* He's so goddamn persistent and it pisses the shit out of me! It's not going to be awkward or anything, just fucking boring, and I don't want to be seen with him. Which is kind of shallow, but it's the truth. No offense, okay?

Well, I guess I'm done wallowing in self-pity.

[*Ana: You need to be more straightforward with people and not care about hurting their feelings. Never feel obligated to do anything that you don't want or have to do, especially if you're just doing it to protect someone's feelings. –J.]

02 September 2008

Running as fast as you can for something that'll fill you with euphoria if you can catch it. I want to push my body as hard as possible. I want to be exhausted when I'm done. I want to punch and kick and scream and tear and become an animal, become a monster writhing in midair with a full screech in my throat, slamming my body into something almost indestructible.

I want my muscles to burst into flames, burning, smoky-thin wisps curling off my body, trailing behind me as I roll on. In victory I curl my fingers into fists, thrust myself into the air, arms reaching, legs pumping, delirious and reeling.

I disappear into the atmosphere.

03 September 2008

Tomorrow is Friday for me because my soccer team is going to Lewiston to play so we are missing school on the real Friday. Today we played a game and won 4-2. I scored thrice, it was sweet.

There is really nothing to say. I've just been thinking about writing my book.

08 September 2008

There is a lot to say. First of all, my high school soccer team went to Lewiston for a couple of games, and the night before we left I spent the night at Lisbet's. We went to Conrad's house with another girl on our team named Bec, and it was super fun! He has a chinchilla because his aunt needed him to take care of it for her, and it basically looks like every animal combined. It looks like a cat and a rat and a bunny and a mouse, and like every rodent ever. So weird.

We smoked out of his homemade gravity bong thing, and did knife hits, and I got very high. For knife hits, you heat up a knife until it's white-hot, and then you press some mota on it and inhale the smoke that it makes. It was weird, but fun. Conrad played his guitar for us and he's fucking incredible. Dead sexy. I'm seriously in love with him. I just wish he weren't high all the time!

We sat in his room and it felt like forever we were in there. There was this one moment that was hilarious only because we were high, and it was when there was this tiny fuzzball in the air and we were trying to keep it afloat by blowing up on it. Conrad lost it in the fan and we were so disappointed, and then we found it again and we were thrilled, and it was ridiculous because the joy on our faces was so visible, glee created by such a minuscule item.

When Lisbet, Bec, and I finally left I had to drive back to Lisbet's house super high. I tailgated her the entire way because I had no idea what was going on and I kept forgetting where I was and losing myself in my thoughts.

When we got to her house we all sat at the kitchen table, and Bec kept making faces at me, and it looked like she was changing into a lot of different people. It was like each feature of her face was from a different person. Then she kept changing into different animals. It was strange.

I don't even know how I managed to wash my face and brush my teeth. I was so out of it. We ended up going to bed at one-thirty a.m. but it felt like it was four a.m.

We had two games in Lewiston and won both. After our second game I went with my parents instead of leaving on the bus to go back home with everyone else. We went out to dinner with Camila and the rest of my family. It was delicious. Dad was being creepy and making dirty jokes with Camila's dad.

The whole time Camila and I texted each other from across the table, arguing about doing Ecstasy because she had a pill and I wanted to split it with her. But we didn't. She scraped off a little from it just so I could taste it. Nothing happened, of course. She's done it, like, twice before and is way more experienced with drugs than me.

We ended up going to her friend's house, and there were about eight people there, all drunk or high, or something. I wished I were, too, but it was fun even though I wasn't. Their friend Joel was there. He's cute, a shaggy-haired stoner. And this girl named Alex, who has great fashion sense. She's skinny and pretty in a bird-like way, and artistic. She has magazine clippings all over her walls, like me!

They are all open-minded and fashionable and I wish I lived there. Sort of. I guess I wish they all lived with me. Especially Camila.

10 September 2008

I don't want to go to school tomorrow. I don't want to be around my parents; they are fucking irritating. Oh, and I especially don't want to go to English tomorrow, because we have to go up in front of the class and talk about whether or not the characters in *Crime and Punishment* are realistic or not.

I think they are. Because how can you say that someone like that isn't real, isn't out there somewhere, isn't possible? You can't. Anything is possible. We are all different, we are anything we want to be. There are billions of people in the world, infinite possibilities, endless scenarios of human experience.

And this fucking idiot girl in my group named Ashley is like, "No, people are not like that. There is no one in the world like Sonya!" I dunno why that pissed me off so bad, but I just wanted to say, "Shut the fuck up, bitch! You know nothing, you can't say that!"

I hate her. I would kill her. She always has this smug grin like she knows she's right. I want to slit her throat and throw her in a ditch to rot. Kick her and spit on her and rip her to shreds. Close my hands around her throat and choke her, strangle her until her lifeless eyes roll into the back of her head and I'll slam her back into the pavement when I'm through.

I find great satisfaction and relief after writing that. It gets it out of my system so I don't actually do it…

15 September 2008

Today school was all right. At lunch Eli and I played ping-pong at his house, and after school, too, because we both had early release.

Sawyer sent us a package today. He's in California now but he was recently in Nevada for the Burning Man festival. It's this huge festival in the middle of the desert where everyone does drugs and parties nonstop for a week or so. In the package were some random items, including this awesome shell necklace and a shawl that he says he used as a "loin-cloth," haha. I'm going to wear it to school tomorrow as a skirt.

16 September 2008

Today the principal at school pulled me aside when we were

going to the stupid "Break Activity" assembly thing, and she told me that my midriff was showing and that I had to go to the nurse to change. I went to the nurse and she was like, "What do you need?" I said, "Mrs. Graham told me to come because of my outfit."

Well, the nurse didn't know what was wrong with my outfit, probably because nothing was wrong with it, so she asked Graham on the walkie talkie. Graham said, "I can see everything but her pubic hair."

In my mind I was like, "WHAT IS GOING ON RIGHT NOW!?" Seriously, what the hell!? If you think about it, that doesn't even make sense! Like, if you could see my vagina, which is really the only thing that shouldn't be showing at school, then you'd have to also see my pubic hair. You wouldn't be able to see everything except for my pubic hair! Like, what??

The nurse just gave me some safety pins to pin my skirt tighter and higher, and then I left.

I fucking hate Mrs. Graham. She's one of those authority figures that completely overuses her power for insignificant reasons.

I feel so out of place. I don't have any group of friends that I actually belong to. I can't see myself hanging out with any of the people I see at school, except for Lisbet, but I don't know if I consider her to be a particularly genuine friend. I don't belong anywhere. I'm such a misfit, and sometimes it makes me sad, but I know I shouldn't be.

Sometimes I really hate my life because it's bland, repetitive, boring, and unexciting. Nothing incredible ever happens. I gladly lose myself in everything I do, everything I watch, everything I read. I want to be friends with people that don't believe one certain thing. People that can't be stereotyped. People that are carefree and not judgmental and drift in the wind like dandelion seeds.

I don't want to hear any more about how Ava got perfect scores on her ACT and SAT. I don't want to hear any more about how Ashley is going to become some amazing author. I don't want to see people as one thing, as one gender, as one emotion. I want them all to open their eyes and see the things around them. I want them to see the sun and feel it on bare arms. I want people to be rational, reasonable, logical. I want the teachers at school to forget the power-hungry mindset.

I want them to see themselves as they really are. I want the people at school to become themselves. I want everybody to be serious and genuine. I want people to hurt and to love and to cry and to laugh and I want people to try new things. And sometimes, maybe not always, I want people to quit over-analyzing and just realize what is truly here.

I want people to stop thinking everything is bad. Everyone is different. There are things people feel and they are so real, regardless of if others understand them.

Maybe I'll never write a book. Maybe I use the same words consistently, rearranged in different forms. Maybe my vocab-ulary isn't as advanced as the rest of my class. But those things don't even matter! What matters is relationships. With others, with yourself. What matters is the little things you do that make you laugh, the character quirks and flaws unique to yourself. The clothes you wear when you're feeling down. Being high, if only once. The taste buds. Being curious about your sexuality.

We all have so many beautiful secrets! There are things I don't even write in here. Everybody should be free. Everyone should run around naked with wild horses and paint on a piece of paper and smell the grass. Lay in it. Lay in the grass. Let the wind move you. Let it grasp your insides, pull them along, throw them into the air.

Let yourself rain down all over everything. Ride a roller coaster. Wish with all your heart that you were something else, and then become it. Become the birds and the trees and the flowers and the moon.

Be the moon, the wise woman that shows you your ignorance. Find that wise woman and tell her everything you feel. Kill fear, do what you want because you don't give a fuck! Lay on the couch all day reading when it's raining outside. And the next day it rains, stay outside until it quits, because variety is the essence of life and you must do everything once.

Sleep all day, stay out all night. Break the rules, be a bad influence. It's good to be bad. Breathe. Inhale your next breath as if it's your last. Listen to your heartbeat. Cradle your stuffed animals. Forget your conscience! Quit being a fucking know-it-all. And lose the need for perfection.

Swim in the ocean, sleep in your swimsuit. Kiss a member of the same sex. Let your nail polish chip and fade away. Write down your ideas and thoughts, because you are a revolutionary. Ignore good advice, then follow it tomorrow. Let time slip past you, laughing. Cry for no reason at all! Do all these things and a million more, and you'll figure out who you are.

19 September 2008

Today is Mom's birthday and we went out to dinner and she opened presents.

I had a game on Wednesday and I scored twice and we won. Conrad saw the game and he texted me later that night saying nice game. It made me feel so good.

20 September 2008

I'm sick. I've been sick all week. I woke up at 11 today. For a while this morning I felt really shitty. Mentally. There are too many things that are categorized and I can't figure them out because everything is everything and I feel so helpless.

There is too much despair and I can't draw or write what I'm thinking. My sentences are ugly and should be rearranged. When I hear things or read them I can't feel anything, but when I watch them I feel it fully. Not knowing what I'd do in certain situations troubles me.

In the movie I watched last night, *The Cell*, this serial killer was abused as a boy and it showed scenes from his childhood, and they were so sick. And I keep thinking, wondering if I had been abused like that, what I would have turned into. I don't think I could have handled it, because I'm always depressed and my life isn't even bad at all. I wonder what I would have thought as a six-year-old being abused. It's all so ugly.

I feel stupid at school. I hate my essay, I can't write shit. I hate school and all the people there. It rained last night and this morning. Everything was moving and the wind was tireless. Nobody's perfect. Pobody's nerfect.

21 September 2008

Yesterday I hung out with Lisbet, Eli, Conrad, and one of Conrad's friends. I slept over at Lisbet's, but before that we all hung out at Conrad's. I smoked and took many a shot of hard alcohol, which I had a bit too much of. We played ping-pong and watched part of this movie called *Orgasmo*, which is super funny because it's about a Mormon porn star.

While we were watching it this guy that was maybe related to Conrad came in and was like, "What are you stoners watching?" Eli and I made eye contact and could read the "OH MY GOD!" in each other's thoughts. We laughed really hard and kept looking at each other because we were all super high and we thought that guy could read minds or something. It was awesome.

I ended up getting way too drunk and I threw up on Conrad's lawn and later in his toilet. But he is so nice, he kept bringing me water and bread and he let me hug him and he made a bed for me in the spare room, although Lisbet and I eventually left. But he took care of me! I think that is sexy.

Then he drove Lisbet and I to her house because there was no way we were gonna drive home; Eli wouldn't let us. Then when we got to her house I passed out in her bed. It felt incredible.

23 September 2008

Today when I woke up I couldn't walk. My ankle was so swollen, I don't know why. I didn't go to school though, which was awesome.

I went to my orthodontist appointment and they took off all the back braces. All the metal bands surrounding my molars are gone, and the brackets on all my back teeth, too. It feels liberating. In two weeks I go back and they'll start making my retainers, and then a week after that I get them all off.

October 14th is the date. Finally. I can't describe how excited I am!

Also, today I saw *Step Brothers* at the dollar theatre with Sawyer, who came home from Cali a while ago. It was pretty funny. Vulgar.

25 September 2008

Yesterday I went to school and I felt really annoying. I don't know why. Just everything I said sounded stupid to me. I didn't play in our game because of my ankle and we lost 4-1.

05 October 2008

I love the song "Liar" by Built to Spill. And the night! I love the night.

14 October 2008

Today is the best day of my life! I got my braces off! Ahhh, it's crazy! I can't even believe it, it's like a miracle. Four fucking years, almost all of high school. My mouth feels weird and slimy. It actually feels strange, like it's not supposed to be like that. I'll just have to get used to it.

On Sunday I hung out with Eli, Lisbet, and Alyssa at the mall, and then we saw *Pineapple Express*, which was a fucking dumb movie. We smoked before we saw it, and it ruined my high terribly. I think I get very critical when I'm high, and the acting starts to look bad and I feel embarrassed for the actors.

17 October 2008

Today is Friday and the week has been so incredibly long. Tomorrow for soccer we have to ride the bus to Lewiston, and I'm going to stay up there with Camila. Then on Sunday I'll drive back to Boise with my parents.

Lately I've loathed myself. I hate my body and my face. But there's nothing I can do so I shouldn't think about it. I feel stupid all the time, but music makes me feel real. Especially Gorillaz. They always make me feel better.

All Eli and Lisbet care about is smoking, and yeah, it's fun, but it's not all there is.

I'm scared of myself. The line between brilliance and insanity is drawn so faintly, everything is everything. Opposites attract, we are all everything else. Drugs aren't bad, they are new levels of perception. There are many people around me but I am so alone. I am scared of myself. I am scared of what I could do on drugs, and just this fact that I am scared means I could have such terrible trips.

Oh, something that annoyed me kind of was Lisbet telling me that some random freshman wrote some really mean shit to Lisbet's mom, who's a teacher at our school, and Lisbet wanted to find her and be a bitch to her. Like tell her she had on an ugly shirt or something. I thought that was immature. Way to be the better person, seriously.

This is the way hate permeates our being. If one would just stop the chain and be kind, the world would be so much better. I wish Lisbet could understand this, but a lot of the time she's immature like that. No offense. I mean, maybe it's reasonable for her to feel that way, because I guess it really hurt her mom's feelings, whatever that girl wrote to her, but I dunno. I wouldn't go to such extra effort to be rude to someone.

21 October 2008

We won our game in Lewiston so we will go to the state tournament. I stayed the night in Lewiston by the way, but I didn't party with Camila because they were only going to drink beer and I hate beer, and I was super tired. I ended up going to bed at 9:30 p.m. But I got to see all my relatives, which was nice. It was fun talking to everyone.

22 October 2008

Today I woke up ten minutes before my alarm went off because I had a nightmare that I was Neo from *The Matrix* and the Mindless Self Indulgence lead singer was trying to kill me.

School was actually not even bad today! It was weird. River sang about AIDS for all of Statistics class. It was so funny, I could not stop laughing. "AIDS, AIDS, AIDS, errybody got AIDS..." I don't think AIDS in general is funny, just the way River was singing it and naming off everybody in class as giving it to everyone else in class was hilarious.

03 November 2008

I can feel the darkness holding the walls together.

04 November 2008

Today is election day. It's official, Barack Obama is our next president!

05 November 2008

I think I'm going shrooming tomorrow. I am super excited! But for some reason I feel like it's going to kill me. Or fuck my brain up so bad that I'll be mentally fucked after. Which really scares me, and I hope nothing bad happens because that would be awful.

I don't think I should worry because tons of people in the world have done shrooms. Indigenous people did, and still do, shit like that for spiritual stuff. I hate when I get like this, it annoys the fuck out of me. I should be taking risks and not giving a fuck because I'm a teenager and a free spirit. It's what young people are supposed to do.

07 November 2008

All right. I can officially say that I have done shrooms. And it was fucking psychedelic! Eli, Lisbet, and I ate them in Lisbet's car outside her sister's apartment. They were gross, dry. I ate them with a plain bagel with nothing on it. We went inside and talked to her sister and her roommates, who hadn't taken shrooms and were going to serve as our trip sitters, and sat on the couch and drank orange juice.

After a while I started feeling weird, like high, sort of. It was strange because I didn't know I would feel high, like with mota. I started to see figures and shapes in the ceiling, and it kind of frightened me.

Then everybody started playing hacky sack outside, and Lisbet and I went to her sister's room, because she has this huge blanket with a mandala on it hanging from the ceiling that serves as a sort of room divider, and we wanted to wave it around to see if it would be trippy. It was.

That's when everything started changing color. I could not figure out what color the dresser was. In reality, it's a yellowish-green color, but it kept shifting hues from yellows to greens to blues and back. A lot of stuff was doing that.

It didn't feel that great to be inside; I got bad vibes. When we went outside, everyone was playing with this soccer ball, and it kept subtly changing shape. It would look really flat and then start to look too pumped up, like air needed to be let out of it.

The colors of the leaves were all more vibrant and beautiful, and when I looked at some leaves close up their outlines seemed to shrivel up and die, and then become colorful again and alive. Everything was dominated by this pulsing, vibrating, breathing effect. There was so much detail and everything looked fuller and more enhanced.

We decided to walk to the park, and it was beautiful. No words to explain. I chased some geese and it was intense when they all flew away because their colors were rich, dark, luscious. The leaves looked plump on the ground like they were hovering about an inch or two in the air.

When we sat down somewhere I looked at the grass up close and I could see it growing. Seriously, sprouting from the ground. It was fucking crazy.

We all talked nonstop about every little thing and I felt like I was in nirvana. As if I knew all there was to know about everything. Like life was some big math equation and we had all figured it out together. I wish I could have had my diary at the time.

I remember I said, "I feel like I need to say this right now: PSYCHEDELIC!" And then I burst out laughing because it felt relevant but so cliché.

I thought about life and how we do things, and that we run

and talk and walk and play because we are all children, and who cares if someone knew we were on shrooms, because I'm still walking and talking like they are. I was just on a different plane of consciousness, like there are many different planes to be on, but we are all in this three-dimensional world and we should all say things that are true, like facts. I felt so happy and I loved everyone, but not in a sexual way.

I got kind of scared though, because I felt like, in reality, I was one of those crazy people on crack that are on the sidewalk dressed in rags mumbling nonsense, and that I just didn't know it. That scared the shit out of me, and I think it was because I wanted to know the truth. Like, why are those people like that? And why am I not one of those people?

My whole life I've only wanted to know the fucking truth, and I can never find it. Or at least it always seems obscure or not as good as I thought it would be.

On the way back to the apartment I was skipping across the sidewalk, and Eli told me to stop because I looked like I was on drugs, and that confused me because I was on drugs, haha. And someone not on drugs could skip, too. I didn't understand why people were insecure and inhibited and why people didn't just do things that made them feel good and happy, without caring if others thought they were stupid or on drugs.

Going back into the city and technology made me feel really bad. Like there were good vibes and bad vibes, and nature created good vibes, and the city center had horrible vibes.

Lisbet had a bad trip. She was running around frantically through the house and kept saying that she needed to go to her dad's house, and she would get in the car and sit there, but then realize that she didn't have her keys or know where they were, so she would come back inside and search for them.

But then she'd forget what she was looking for and freak out because she felt crazy.

At one point she asked me if her eyes were bleeding. I looked into them and all I saw was fear, and she wasn't in there.

I started to get worried that my parents would find out and that I'd get in a lot of trouble, and that I was super ugly like those people on meth whose faces are fucked up. I thought I was one of them, and it was the worst feeling ever. So I laid on the bed and then Lisbet came in looking frightened, and she started taking her shirt off. I told her to stop because in the back of my mind I knew that for some reason that was not a good idea.

Her sister's cat crawled up to us and I was petting it for the longest time. It felt wonderful, peaceful. I was astounded that such a beautiful creature could exist and that it wanted to interact with me.

Eventually the high wore off.

God, I can't stop thinking about it! It was like I was in a different world, or like I had another sense or something. I could really connect with plants and animals, and I could feel positive and negative vibes in various places. Everything had a sort of spirituality, a personality that I could sense that I had never perceived before. Jesus. What a fuckin' thought!

Oh, about things changing color: things that are the same color change to a different color at the same time, and they change to the same color. So everything has a kind of pattern to it, and it's lovely and strange. You get caught up in and overwhelmed by the complexity and futility of every part of life. It feels philosophical, psychological. If you let it, it can get scary. Like a nightmare you can't wake up from.

You get confused about why people do certain things because there's no point in doing anything. Like me writing all this, there's absolutely no point. There's no reason why we are alive and moving and perceiving. It just happened, with an explosion of energy, and there's nothing you can do about it. Yet, in the same moment, if you let yourself enjoy it and stop worrying, it becomes fun and exciting.

You may start thinking about being crazy, and it's also confusing because what the fuck is "crazy" anyway? We all have different opinions, and we all do different things that make us happy. We all interact with other people. It's like each person interacts with her kind of person, and everyone is different. Everybody is a little insane, but nobody knows it. Everyone knows what she is talking about, but if she is misunderstood she is called crazy.

Life seems to be about connecting with people and finding things that make us feel good. And saying words that make us feel good, even if they don't make sense. Because for me, nothing makes sense, but at the same time, everything makes sense.

You just have to surround yourself with people that understand you. Which is strange because there is no standard of what makes sense. There are many different perspectives about the same situation. There can't seem to be a right and wrong to me regarding understanding or meaning.

Lisbet was not saying things that were true, and this is something that confuses me because it seems like it is wrong, but is it? She thought I was Eli, and she kept asking if her friend Ben was there, and he wasn't. He hadn't been with us at all that day. She also thought she was her sister for a while, and that Eli was a really bad person. He was using her sister's computer and she got bad vibes from him and wanted him to leave the room.

There were very irrational fears, very irrational thoughts, but at the same time, the thoughts had meaning. I would say weird things, or have vastly different ideas that weren't related at all, one right after the other, but that's actually how I felt at the time, so it was true. I could also tell when I looked at something that it wasn't real, like the colors, and I could see what normal people would see, but then I let the shrooms change me because it was more interesting.

We would call things by names that were not the correct names. Like, I called the dresser a desk, but it was okay because everything is everything, nothing has a name, it has a feeling, a personality. It's okay to not be so specific when speaking English.

We were all each other because we were united. That was a great feeling. I felt united with nature and the world and the atmosphere. We were listening to the band CocoRosie, and those vibes were intensely right. That music was perfect for a shroom trip. I think it's important that I experienced all that.

I've thought of another thing: shrooms, I think, kind of strip away language and leave only feeling. I sort of think that the reason Lisbet got scared and was mean to Eli and freaking out and wanting her dad is because she feels insecure deep down inside.

Like, she needs her family, her father, someone to protect her, but a lot of the time she hides this. She covers this fact and makes fun of other people, brings them down because it makes her feel better, knowing that she's not as bad off as they are. Knowing that she has better qualities than them. It's like she can't accept those things in herself so she distracts

84

herself by highlighting negative things in other people's lives.

[*Ana: You would love Terence McKenna. –J.]

10 November 2008

I woke up late today because I set my alarm for p.m. instead of a.m. I didn't get lunch detention for being late though, because the guy let me off. It was crazy. And basically that's all this day has been good for. It was just school. Blah blah blah. I have soccer at eight tonight. I'm done with all my homework.

12 November 2008

I'm constantly thinking, processing, analyzing. Information is always flowing into my brain. When I hear people talk I try to only listen to the voice, the tone, the pitch, and not what they are saying, and it is arduous! I cannot not know what they are talking about. It bothers me.

I can't concentrate anymore at school. Everything we do is so tedious. I have to do all this shit that I don't want to do, that I don't care about. I don't know why I don't just lay on the ground and die. Just collapse. I don't know how to do my Statistics or Economics homework.

I hate living with my parents, it really irritates me. I want to be alone, and I want to know all the things. I want to be pretty, I want to kill Ashley in my English class and this stupid Mason kid in my government class. He thinks he is so mature, so knowledgeable. Fuck him, fuck school. Fuck everything, and everyone who thinks he knows himself.

I hate when people analyze shit and how people act and who

people are. And I encompass all of these things. None of this matters. The past clogs the present and the future. I wish people would forget everything once the day was over. I wish I weren't human, susceptible to everything. It's demoralizing.

I wish Conrad liked me. I hate that I wish Conrad liked me. I hate my stomach and my love handles. I'm the only one that knows myself. When I'm alone I am truly me. At school I am only a shadow of the reality within. I am a different person around each different person. Eli is the only one who is closest to me. But he hangs out with Lisbet more than me, smokes mota every day; it's all he cares about.

Why do people go to so much trouble to feel strongly about something? Like politics. Like many of the world's affairs. I want to die and never have to put up with this shit. With hope, with being let down, with disappointment, with self-loathing, with awkwardness. It's all such a disease.

I write for myself. Myself!

15 November 2008

Yesterday I put my music on in the garage and juggled my soccer ball for, like, an hour. It was relaxing, I really enjoyed it.

Eli came over later and we hung out in my room and I made us some hemp jewelry. We made playlists for him and talked about the future and about him and the girl he likes, and just everything. We had tea and food, and it was the greatest time. I absolutely love having conversations with him. It's good to connect with someone that shares my ideas and beliefs. Well, not all of them, but there's always going to be things that people disagree on. I had a great time.

We are all so abused. The one you love never loves you back. I talk simply and it fills me with rage. I can't find enough verbs and nouns and my sentences are boring. All I ever say to express myself is fuck! Fuck, fuck, fuck, it's all I ever feel, all I ever say. It's useless and ugly and plain.

I absolutely loathe being a girl. It's unfair. Teenagers are always figuring themselves out, I think. I just hate the things I say sometimes. And I feel so ugly. Always I'm ugly, red, oily, huge nose. I hate it. I hate everything.

Everyone in the whole world is infected with ugliness. There are rude vibes permeating everything I hear. All I can think about is whether what I just said was annoying or stupid in the minds of the people I'm around. I'm so self-conscious. I hate myself so much sometimes, but I'm extremely good at keeping it hidden inside myself.

You're the only one I can talk to, is that stupid? Except for Eli, but I sound like I'm fishing for compliments when I talk about this with him.

The people on my soccer team are super rude sometimes. All they care about is drinking and smoking and I think there are lots of other cool things to do, but no one knows this.

I wish I could wake up in an expansive field of lush, green grass. Green like the color of summer and fresh limes. It goes on for miles. An ocean of green, horizon contrasting sharply with the blue atmosphere. There is nothing but my imagination.

I open my eyes and all I see are white, block letters. "The earth is yours." No one but me. I rise and stand on my feet and turn. Around and around, I break into a jump, a leap. I sprint as fast as I can. Legs, lungs, heart, breath, arms; all throbbing, pumping, living, pushing.

23 November 2008

Today I saw *Twilight* with Mom, and it was *so* cheesy. The characters had no personalities; it was boring. But it was also hilarious because we were too embarrassed for them and we could not stop laughing in the theatre. We almost had to leave because we couldn't be quiet. The whole time we were like, "Seriously, you guys? Are you really taking this seriously!?" And everybody else in the theatre was so absorbed.

27 November 2008

Today is Thanksgiving, and I am leaving for a soccer tournament in California, with my club team. High school soccer's been over for a while now. We lost at the start of the state tournament.

29 November 2008

California. I could sit out on this balcony for hours and hours and hours. Across from us is a tall hotel with many rooms lit up, and there are tiny people moving about in them, looking out the windows and doing random things. The sky is dark and cloudy in the night. There are lights everywhere on all the buildings. Cars drive by on the open streets, trains are a regular occasion. People walking on the sidewalk so far down look miniscule.

The way I feel about everything is so important. Living, breathing, full of spirit. A myriad of noises: boats and sirens and people yelling, and I love it so much. I don't want to go back home, back to school. It's going to be ugly and depressing.

01 December 2008

Back from California. School wasn't horrifying today. I was dwelling on the futility of it all, life I mean, in the shower. I always feel like I have to be getting things done and out of the way, and crossed off my lists. It makes me kind of anxious, I realized.

I was thinking about how eating and showering and sleeping take up so much time when I have homework to do, and then I was thinking, what if I didn't have homework? Would I just not do anything? Would I only exist to exist, with no purpose, living on and on, feeling hatred and irritation and fear for my whole life?

Everything is useless, and rude too, just existing and taunting me. Then I thought about killing myself because there's no point for me to be here, and that really scared me. It was such an irrational fear, too, which also scared me because I don't want to go crazy, letting things that aren't going to hurt me or even happen scare me and control my mind.

Another thing I have been worrying about is that I feel like I can't concentrate, like I can't pay attention in my psychology class. I get distracted easily and my mind wanders and I feel stupid all the time. Sometimes I just can't think. God, I worry too much. I get it from Mom, I think.

02 December 2008

I was watching the National Geographic channel today and it was about heroin addictions and drugs, and it really scared me. I feel like I'm going to do these drugs and then turn into one of those people walking on the street in rags and all dirty, trying to get enough money for another high.

When those people do those drugs they don't care about society. Like, they are dressed half naked and they don't even care. It looks bad to us, to normal people. But is it inherently bad? Because it isn't to people on drugs…but they are on drugs. But it's like they are just on a different level of consciousness, and everything is an opinion so it can't be bad, but it clearly is!

All this scares me because I can't figure it all out. Sometimes I feel like I need to be a strong-willed person and prove to people that I can do these drugs only once, but there are people that try to do just that and fail miserably. I know I would be no different. I'm still curious though, which is the stupid thing, because I know I wouldn't be able to conquer myself like that.

I guess I need to accept the fact that I'm human, therefore weak, and I'm never going to do addictive drugs like heroin or meth or whatever. I also want to remember that I never need to do things I don't want to do. I don't have to do drugs to be accepted. I don't need to prove myself to anyone. I don't need to succumb to peer pressure. I feel better getting that off my chest.

But still there's this feeling deep down that consists of fear and anxiety and sadness. Maybe I'm imagining it. I don't know why I feel this way. I don't think it's bad or anything; it's probably just a phase. I have phases that I worry about occasionally and I need to relax because it's probably nothing. It's perfectly human and normal to feel sad or depressed. I need to stop feeling like what I am doing or feeling is bad or not right somehow. I am a young adult, I'm finding myself, and it's healthy.

I think a lot of the time I can't figure out what's good or bad because I try to see everything as beautiful and a part of life. But being addicted to heroin isn't beautiful. At the same time, it is, though. Succumbing to something greater than yourself, letting it destroy you. It's terrifying, but beautiful. It's horrible, yet beautiful.

I just need to decide which routes I want to take, and that is not one of them.

05 December 2008

I think we are all beautiful. And whatever we feel is beautiful, because we are sensing so many things. It doesn't matter if what we feel is illogical or silly or terrible; it's all real and human, so it's lovely. Our release of these emotions is a harmonious song of life, good or bad.

If we make music to express our feelings, it is wonderful. Even when people say awful things that make us want to cry, it's beautiful because this raw sensation of being is evoked. We are responding to stimuli and it's weird and luscious.

But I loathe it sometimes, and there are ugly parts, too, but I can't decide if these really are ugly parts or if I think everything is lovely. And tomorrow I'll probably have a different opinion.

06 December 2008

Eli and I rode bikes downtown and met up with some of his friends, and did two drug deals. He's selling mota to these young kids, it's hilarious.

While we were downtown I kind of had a mental breakdown. I cried in the park and told Eli my worries and fears. I thought I was insane for a while. The trees were just too bare, the silence too loud, the sky too gray and looming, and I freaked out. Eli told me that my mind gets inside of itself too much. I think he's right. I wouldn't like to talk about it anymore, actually.

I had pizza at his house, homemade. We hung out in his room while it was cooking. I made a hemp anklet while he played his guitar. It felt all right.

08 December 2008

Oh my fucking god. Today in English we presented these random projects about *Lord of the Flies*, and I want to kill myself now because it was so horrible. I just read off the poster, and when we had to talk about the "Stages of Moral Development" of the characters in the book, I totally did not know what I was talking about, because I had not reviewed it, and I felt like a fucking dumbass and I could tell that my face got super red.

It was awful. Let's never speak of it again, I want to forget the whole thing. I hate when embarrassing things happen and then you can't stop thinking about it. All right. Amnesia...

Hello. My name is Ana and I love to breathe. I am not better than you, or worse. I have an appetite for adventure, which remains unsatisfied because I live in a world where nothing exciting ever happens. There are no accessible strange planets with life forms unique to them, or beautiful people who talk about things other than drugs, who fly spaceships into other worlds to save their friends. There are no adventures here. All

I have for that are books and movies, and I loathe that I cannot be one of the people I read about.

My world is consumed by school, which is long and monotonous and I learn about things I don't care about and the people are rude and unlike me and I can't connect with them. I hate it so much; my whole being is consumed with pointless loathing. But there are times when my world can be satisfactory. We have great sunsets, even though we only have one sun.

In the summer when the grass is green and soft and the air warms my body, I feel happy. Right now the bare trees are mysterious and pretty, and the air is bitingly cold. Hot cups of coffee and lullabies in a bookstore where everything smells crisp and new. Opinions. A smile, however fleeting. Clothes to pretend you are something else, when really you're all of it. It doesn't have to be sane. We can all be uneasy babies walking around immersed in technology, or we can listen to all that is around us.

I'll feel what you have to say through poetry and writing, and the quietness of the library will shove me into this diary, and I'll write and write and write until there's nothing left to say, and then I'll cry because the futility of it all makes me feel insane, and it's scary. The whole world can be scary sometimes, and I want to press my thumbs to my temples so hard that my brain will squish out and I won't have to exist anymore.

Yet, existence can be fascinating. When I look at everything it's either fat or skinny. Correctness is a fallacy. Let's push boundaries. Let's be cowardly and bold and shrink into the ground and slink away into a forest to hide among all the people I wish were real.

All of the time I want to have interesting things to say when people converse with me, but usually I make a fool of myself. I'm bad at communicating, but at least I know that. I do know things, it just seems like I don't when I try to explain it to other people. I think explaining is difficult. But it's all okay because at least I know what I'm thinking.

12 December 2008

I write because there's something I need to say. But as more words appear on paper, the farther I am from my subject. It's like I try to find the meaning of life and write it down in one, moving sentence, but it's impossible, and I feel crazy sometimes trying to figure it out.

I'm reading *The Bell Jar*. It's supposed to be about the protagonist's gradual descent into insanity, which is interesting. But it's weird because she says some things that perfectly describe how I think. Like, one time when she was feeling low, she felt like all these distressing intuitions she had about herself were coming true. And that is exactly how I feel so many times.

Like, sometimes I secretly think that in the future I'll go crazy, or kill myself, or kill somebody else, and other random things that I don't recall right now. There's just something inside me that knows one of these things is going to happen, but at the same time, I don't believe it. It's unnerving sometimes.

13 December 2008

I made an appointment at Paul Mitchell for the 31st. Jenna is going to school there and is going to color my hair, and I'll get the "model fee" so it will be cheaper. I want to bleach it blonde and put cool colors in it.

18 December 2008

I'M UGLY.

20 December 2008

I feel like I don't have anything to say anymore. Today was shitty. I was in a bad mood all day and all I did was go shopping with Mom. I was supposed to start my period a week ago and I still haven't. I shouldn't be that worried about it though, since I've never had sex.

I haven't been eating very well, because nothing ever sounds good and I'm never hungry. I haven't been writing as much because I'm afraid of you. Me. I dunno. There are so many different reasons. I can't think of any right now, probably a good thing.

21 December 2008

I went to Eli's house and hung out. We were going to see *Burn After Reading* at the dollar theatre, but Mom wouldn't let me drive because of the slick roads. Oh, well. We watched *The Matrix* so it was all right.

I think Eli's younger brother likes me sometimes, because he always starts conversations with me at school, and once when there was a fire drill outside in the cold, he gave me his sweatshirt. And he brings that up in conversations sometimes, and brings up past things I've said that I forgot I said. And today at Eli's house he was following us around, and it was weird.

Maybe I am completely misinterpreting all of this. Hmm…

23 December 2008

Today Sawyer arrives! We have to get him at the airport in about an hour. Tomorrow is Christmas Eve. The days are flying by. Last night I dreamt that River and Phil and I (Phil is this random kid from Statistics) were in a band together, and we were doing a show and people booed us. I wrote lyrics and Phil completely changed them and I was pissed. It was weird.

26 December 2008

After skiing today with my family, in the car on the way home, Dad drove fast, and on the corners I leaned toward the window and it felt like we were going to flip the car. Over and over until our souls shattered and the car exploded with fire and flame and lights, and we'd be spread over the entire universe; we could be the entire universe.

At the end of the day my hands were frozen and my toes were ice, so I went into the lodge before everyone else and got a hot chocolate and a cookie, and sat with my parents' friend and her niece. One of Sawyer's friends saw me and asked me to come sit with her and her little sister and eat nachos.

I declined because I didn't know if it would be rude to leave the people I was already with. Then I felt really awkward and dumb because I wasn't doing anything and they were sitting at a table close to ours. Oh, well. Story of my fucking life. Whoever I am.

There's you, and then there's your brain, the route through which you function. It gets in the way.

I try to think of my actions as cool, like when you meet someone different, new, and exciting, and you think everything they do is wonderful and creative and strange. It's hard to do, but I try. I try to think of myself as interesting, like I'm just meeting myself.

27 December 2008

As much as I try to deny this, a person can feel so much better when they find another person to relate to or seek guidance from. I try to be self-reliant most of the time, but it does feel good to find outside advice instead of listening only to your own coaxing voice inside your head. I don't know why, but it's hard for me to ask for help.

Just telling my mom that I think I'm depressed (which I did today) made me super uncomfortable. I don't know what's wrong with me. But she gave me two books to read about depression, and for some reason that professional tone and tiny font made me feel way better, like everything would turn out okay, and I'd be able to smile and have it be genuine.

I started reading *The Perks of Being a Wallflower* and it makes me feel reassured because I feel like the boy in many ways. He is such a beautiful person, with sincere feelings and interesting thoughts. Also, I feel reassured because it is written in a diary type form. The entries are actually letters but it's similar to how I want to write my book.

I think it would be neat to actually be a published author. I think that would be so cool. It makes me feel excited.

28 December 2008

Okay, I wanted to write a book, but I dunno if I want to do

that anymore, because I'd have to edit too many people's names and it wouldn't really be a story like *The Perks of Being a Wallflower*, and nothing interesting or bad ever happens to me. But I guess it might be interesting to other people. I dunno. I could make stuff up, too, I'd just have to keep things straight, which will probably be hard to do, but I dunno. You have to work at everything you do, don't you?

29 December 2008

I can't stop thinking about how mind-boggling everything is. And how we feel things like fear, and how fear is only a word but the actual feeling is insane because you can't see it or touch it, but you know it's there and it's so weird. There are all these other feelings that I get but they don't have names and I can't define them, and this terrifies me for some reason.

These feelings are vibes I get from the things around me. Like tea and incense and meditation and Buddhism and writing and photography and music. They all have vibes that make me feel this certain way that has no explanation. It makes me feel good, but that is so broad, general, vague.

The way nature looks at you. Different seasons, variations of plants and animals, they all affect my consciousness and I don't know why and I can't explain. These feelings are hanging around me at all moments, like curtains on a window. It bothers me because I wish I could be the feeling, not have to feel it. I wish I could be the curtain, not the window.

I feel like I'm supposed to be feeling a certain way, like I am supposed to be happy and go to school and get along with everyone and get good grades and be successful and not make mistakes. I hate this. I feel like I need to mess something up in such grandeur that I can just…I don't know. I don't know. I don't know. There's something there but I don't know what it is.

I am unhappy. I am depressed. I wonder if I have depression. Only thinking about how I am human and I sense things scares me, because my mind is jammed with all these fears and worries and I can't get them out. Death seems to be the only answer. But suicide is sad. My parents and friends would be devastated. Maybe. I dunno.

Writing it out is a type of definition of my emotions, so I hope I feel better, because I do kind of feel better. I'm not sure if I do, though, because I can't figure myself out sometimes, which is another thing that scares me. It is because I do not know who I am. Or maybe it is because I do not know what I am. Because there is your brain, and then there is you. They're separate. But what exactly are you? What is it when you use "I" as a word for yourself?

And everything is so pointless. What we do doesn't matter one bit, because in the end we all die, cease to exist. And after that nothing happens. It's like falling asleep, you aren't aware of yourself because you are not there. You just are not a thing anymore, you're gone.

The worst thing about all of this is that nothing is actually wrong with me. Because nothing bad has ever happened to me that could trigger a mental disorder. None of my friends have killed themselves. I have a home life that is perfectly normal and fine. My parents are good people. I am not abused in any way. All this pisses me off even more because I feel like I have no right to feel bad, ever, and I do, so I feel that I am wrong.

I think I create these terrible feelings for myself because of a lack of anything bad in my life to give me these feelings naturally. I just feel like all these bad things are going to happen to me, like I'm going to go insane and kill myself. I don't know why.

30 December 2008

We are spirits trapped in cages, our minds encased in a body, a head. Only when we die and break out of these cages will we really be in tune with all that is around us: nature, animals. The animals are our spirits, previously humans, trapped in bodies. They do not concern themselves with us because we do not matter.

We are truly alone; we cannot be with another person truly because our spirits do not touch. But in death we will see everything truly and become one with everyone else, all else, the earth, the atmosphere.

People take drugs to feel this sense of unity, but it is all false, although interesting.

31 December 2008

Today I went to Paul Mitchell to get my hair done by Jenna. And I hate it. It took six hours to get the black out (I know, dying my hair black with box dye was a bad idea), and now it's orangish blonde, more reddish. And my hair is dead and broken. It was long and exhausting to participate in, and also painful because my hair was being uncooperative and tangly. Jenna cried at the end, too, because it was so much work and super frustrating.

I did get about four inches off and layers, though. I'm going back in on Friday so they can make my bangs, and I dunno if

I'm going to be able to put crazy colors in it anymore, because nothing'll match and my hair is already damaged enough.

01 January 2009

Today I got up, had some coffee, and decided to go on a walk, because today was one of those gray, calm, timeless days where it's as if no one exists but you. So I walked and looked at the trees and the grass and pondered on my sanity.

I was walking through this tiny little park, and I heard this pattering of running feet, so I turned around and I saw this small, white, black, and gray spotted dog. He jumped up on me, and he had a tennis ball so I threw it and he brought it back to me. And we played fetch for the longest time.

It was fun, but after a while I felt like he didn't truly love me, he only loved his ball, so I left. He followed me and then went into some random people's garage, and I told them that he wasn't mine and we talked for a bit.

I thought about humans being morphing bodies, growing, changing. Traveling through time, never constant. Time is simply a path you cannot stop on, or turn around on. Memory is the only way to visit the past.

I am in love with Gorillaz. They are perfect and lovely and they always make it better.

02 January 2009

I now have bangs. They have blue on the underside, a navy blue, but I think once I shower it'll be lighter and look different, but I don't think it'll look bad. I love them. I didn't think I would. It's so much different than the first day they did it.

It's unusual having bangs when I've believed for my whole life that they were impossible because of my cowlick. And now it's hidden!

I bought a moisture kit thing with shampoo, conditioner, and hairspray. It was $31.80, which is a lot, but I thought I'd buy one because Jenna needed to sell them to be able to go on one of their trip things. And it would be a thank you for doing my hair, which I absolutely love.

04 January 2009

I have soccer in half an hour. I am nervous and excited. I am super out of shape so it'll probably suck, but oh well. I hope I don't get too frustrated, because it puts me in the worst mood.

Tomorrow I have to go back to school; Christmas break is basically over. It's going to be the worst time of my life. I'm laying down in the living room listening to "Slow Country" by Gorillaz. Awesome bass, beautiful.

08 January 2009

I loathe this ignorant world. I feel like there is something more than this lame human existence. This feeling to me is like knowing there is another way you could sense something, but not being able to sense it. Like being born blind and knowing that you can't see things; it probably is such an irritation! To know of its existence but not be able to experience it.

I feel like meditation and Buddhism and wisdom and enlightenment are the paths to being able to understand this thing that haunts me, but I feel like I'm too confused to get involved in that shit. Like, I haven't set my priorities straight and they won't accept me. I feel like I'm too impatient or sensitive or over-reactive.

Yoda didn't want to train Luke at first because he didn't focus on the present moment; he was too impatient. So I feel like someone wouldn't want to train me. I wish I had a Yoda to guide me to wisdom.* I feel like nothing adventurous or exciting like *Star Wars* or other action and adventure movies will ever happen to me, only because I want it to, and I daydream about it and think about it and write about it all the time.

[*Ana: You don't need a teacher. You are your own guru. Sit in a chair. Close your eyes. Breathe deeply in and out, slowly. Visualize your breath cleansing your chakras. Start by doing this 15 minutes a day. Research the chakras and visualization techniques. –J.]

Maybe someday something sensational will happen to me. I just feel held back here. Like I'm in a cage and I can't get out.

The world is about feeling, and we are bodies of feeling that need to learn to throw these feelings away. Let them flow away, let them consume. Release them like the trees' release of leaves in the fall and winter. It can be done in any number of ways. It's fulfilled in those moments where you don't think, where you act on instinct, or when your mind is clear during meditation or sleep.

For me, soccer gives me this way of releasing energy. I am just a body of action, of movement, of sinew and meat, of bones and hair and skin, acting as one fluid unit. This is where I forget my mind and let my primal nature dominate. I let my lust for force and strength and the conquering of fears control my body. All of these feelings flow through me. I am the feeling in these moments. I am the feeling in these moments!

Music. I can feel it in the air, gushing and throbbing, pulsating around me. Noise matching my own heartbeats. It becomes me, fills in those parts of me I didn't know were empty. Not empty, just unfulfilled.

21 January 2009

I went to Portland for a soccer tournament. The girl I roomed with talks in her sleep and rolls around and lays on you, so I got no sleep. One night she was like, "What? What did I do? I didn't do anything!" It was weird.

It was really cold there. The first day we had one game and we tied. The second day we had two games, won one and lost one. I felt like such an idiot in the game we lost. And it was early and fucking cold, and the team wasn't even good at all.

23 January 2009

We are put into this world where possibilities are limitless, where you can move and speak to other people, and cause them to feel certain things, and it's all so unbelievable. You can do whatever you want!

But everybody is chained to their morals and authority and chained to their own mind's constraints. I say fuck it all. I say do whatever you want, what makes you feel amazing. Don't listen to what others think; be yourself, do things your way. If someone thinks you're stupid, fuck them. (Lol, don't literally fuck them, just say "fuck you" to them.)

I can think all these things, write all these things, but opinions aren't truth. What I think may change tomorrow, or in five minutes, or right after I write it down. That's why you can never judge people. Do what you want, but don't hurt people because everyone is beautiful and precious.

However, sometimes you have to destroy something beautiful. Build something up and then tear it down. Life is feeling. Make yourself feel infinite, like Charlie in *The Perks of Being a Wallflower*. Immortal, crazy in a remarkable way. Versatility. Man, woman. Let it all go, hit bottom.

29 January 2009

River from school is making these cool scarves for his clothing line that he wants to create, and I got to model them. He's giving me one for only five dollars. Sophie, River's friend who looks like Frankenstein's bride or a trans pin-up girl, took pictures of me posing and I probably looked really ugly, but whatever.

At school we've been working on our senior projects. Mine's on the *Death With Dignity Act* in Oregon. It's not that hard. School's stupid.

Today I wore a black poofy dress and someone told me that I looked like I had just walked off the set of a My Chemical Romance music video. Goth prom, that's the look I was going for, I guess.

I don't want to go to sleep. I don't want to have to sleep. I want to do origami and read, and play backgammon and Uno, and read magazines and be an adult and wear outfits like Marla Singer, and go shopping at the farmer's market, and not be too cold, and I don't want the sun to shine too much. I want it to be springtime. I don't want things to be so normal and neat and straight like everything here.

01 February 2009

Today I went skiing with Dad and we met up with Sawyer and Lacy, who is Sawyer's sort of girlfriend. She has long blonde hair and talks more than anyone I've ever met. She's really nice, I like her. It was cold but I used hand warmers so it was okay. But my feet froze. We left early so we could watch the Super Bowl. I didn't watch it because I hate football.

This coming weekend I go to Seattle for my official college visit, and I'll meet the other recruits. I'm nervous but I can handle it. I hope I can make friends with them easily. And I don't even know how to make friends.

Tomorrow I have school, which is shitty.

04 February 2009

Today after school Sawyer and I went to a coffee shop and I did my Statistics homework. We played backgammon and I beat him thrice in a row. We got refillable mugs of coffee and I drank three cups.

05 February 2009

I feel really weird right now. Like a bad alone feeling. I feel like my pulse is faster than normal, and I don't know who I am, and what is all this shit that's surrounding me? These machines, living things, sunlight, escalator stairs.

I'm going to be meeting people I don't know, in Seattle. It's our official visit, when the new soccer recruits will meet each other and the whole team will be together for the first time. What will we talk about? In reality, we are truly alone…inside our own bodies, inside our own minds and thoughts.

Mom's gone and I'm sitting at my gate at the airport alone, feeling nervous and jittery, not liking who I am, who I've been. I feel so bland sometimes, like everyone else has their particular niches, their good friends they're always with, and I don't have anyone. Or anything. I'm not as cultured as the people I know. I don't know who I want to be, what group I want to belong to.

I keep thinking about how I won't be able to figure out where to go or what to do, that I'll just break down and fall to the ground, helpless. People will stare and be freaked out, and then I'll truly be alone. Physically instead of mentally. I feel like I won't be able to find food and water, and friends. I feel helpless and hopeless. Then I wonder if I'm making this all up.

08 February 2009

Tomorrow is school. I am back from Seattle! We went to a fancy restaurant the first night for dinner, and I met my fellow recruits. They're all pretty nice. We drove around a lot with the current freshmen on the team and hung out in the dorms. We also went to the women's basketball game.

But the best part was that we went to a party and got drunk and it was kickass! At the party the cops eventually came and told the underage people to walk home, so we did. It was awesome. I am happy they drink. Drinking is prohibited on campus because it's a private Christian school. One girl on the team had mota, too. I guess not all of them are religious, thankfully.

I had to get up at eight this morning to go to the airport, and I had a slight hangover. I looked out the wall of windows there and watched the planes take off, and ate this delicious breakfast burrito, and everything was okay. Then when I got home I took a four-hour nap.

God, I am excited to go there; I can't wait! I think it's all going to be all right.

12 February 2009

Lately I feel like I've been thinking that things are impossible, or just unlikely to occur, so what's the use in trying? Or believing? For example, I'd like to write a book, but it's probably unlikely to be a good one, and it takes too much time, so I feel like it's impossible.

When things don't happen in a short span of time I feel like they're useless. I guess I've been feeling like things are pointless. I dunno, it's all very confusing.

I'm trying to figure out who I am, I'm trying to like who I am. I'm trying to accept myself, get good vibes from how I'm sitting and what I'm wearing. But I just end up getting sick of myself.

I want to be a certain thing. I don't want to be everything anymore because I can't define myself. I want to be Angelina Jolie, or the gunslinger. I'm directionless. A wanderer with no purpose. I want weird and crazy and unbelievable things to happen to me (without drug use) but I'm having a hard time believing these are possible, which pisses me off.

I'm struggling with my consciousness, the subjectivity of reality and truth, good and evil, right and wrong. I don't know what I believe. I want to believe in something but nothing continues to happen. It's really quite frustrating. I've got to come to terms with my opinions. Recognize that I like and dislike things.

Today I broke through my wall. I conquered my personal demon. I ran for 50 minutes. It was tiring, but near the end I pushed through and I felt like I had more energy, so I'm declaring today as my "passage past breaking point." Hitting bottom, you know? It's all about enlightenment. I'm going to lose myself every time I run because it feels right. It's a way of release, a way of slicing yourself open and leaving everything behind. Emptiness.

Tomorrow's Friday the 13th. I hope something bad happens so I can fucking deal with it.

24 February 2009

Blah. Soccer sucked today, I feel weirdly insecure. I just want to be alone. I'm at the public library, going to check out some movies. I did my Statistics, which is nice. I think I'm gonna go, I don't feel like writing anymore.

07 March 2009

Haven't written in what feels like forever. I had vivid, colorful dreams last night. I regret waking up. We were walking down these stone stairs on the side of a mountain that were super tall, and the view was of the ocean, spread out to the left, all shimmery and glittering and neon multicolored. The stairs ended in the water, which was warm, soft, soothing, shallow.

All these sea creatures started splashing, making the whole ocean burst and break, reflecting the sun at a billion different angles. The creatures, upon closer inspection, were actually paper origami creations. We picked them up out of the water and put our mouths around a corner of each one. When we blew air into them they unfolded into varying shapes.

Eventually, the sun began setting and it turned the clouds a vibrant orange and deep purple-blue. Like the colors of smeared blueberries and blackberries and orange peels. We were up there in the clouds, flying around, and then someone was kayaking in the clouds, and another person was riding a surfboard. I sat down on the surfboard and was riding it, but then I couldn't see anything and they told me to stop and I hit a wall or something…and then I woke up.

16 March 2009

Last night I got back from our tournament in Las Vegas. We won three games and lost one, and the teams there weren't that great. I don't feel like I played that well. I think I'm in a rut sort of. My touches are off, I don't look around to see if I have time, and I don't feel composed.

I'm scared for college. I feel like I'm not going to be as good as the other girls. I'm way nervous. I'm trying to be carefree and go with the flow and not worry about things, but it's really hard.

Lately I just feel fat, or wide, or bigger than everybody else. It's ridiculous because I know I'm not. I need to relax; I'm not overweight.

21 March 2009

It's officially spring break! Last night Sawyer and Lacy and I went to Lacy's friend's house and drank alcohol. I smoked mota too, the first time in forever. We played this card game called Asshole and played darts.

Eventually we went to this bar and I tried to get in with Lacy's old ID, and the bouncer was like, "This looks nothing like you." He asked me the birthday, which I knew, and then the zip code, and I was like, "Uhhh…" I felt so stupid, and he took the ID and wouldn't give it back to me, and Sawyer was like, "Fuck!" So we left.

We went to the foothills and climbed up to the top of the main hill in the dark that you can access from the park. It was around one in the morning, and we could hear a few other people somewhere in the blackness. City lights burning stars into the empty space of night. I always think about how those lights signify the lives of thousands of people I'll never know, how they are moving to rhythms so different from my own, and how maybe they are thinking about the same things I do.

I also think about how I am in that moment, during that moment. Like, when I am mesmerized by the lights of civilization, cradled by the thick underwing of darkness, I think about how I am there and how that moment encompasses my being. I am that moment. It's important.

Oh, I also want to say this: last night when I was a little drunk and maybe high, there was a moment when we were playing darts that I got scared, of life, of being crazy, of what I'm going to do with my life, who I am. Weird shit like that. I hate when this fear takes over me because I feel like I'm going to die or something, and I'm confused, and I feel like I'm insane.

I felt really alone, because in reality, we are all alone. Inside our own heads, and even when you're talking with someone you are still separate from each other. There's not a complete connection, a cable of understanding, and when you're drunk or high or on drugs, these cables of understanding and connection are altered and twisted. Sometimes it can make you feel even more alone and confused. It's depressing and frightening. If I think about it too much I freak myself out.

25 March 2009

We had a tournament last weekend and it was lame. The teams were bad and we won by a lot every time. After our last game we came home so I could shower, and then Mom and Sawyer and I drove to Lewiston.

I had texted Conrad a lot the day before I left because he called me when I was drunk with Sawyer and Lacy. I texted him a lot the next day, too, because I was watching *Twilight* with Jenna and it was super annoying and boring. But anyway, I'm in love with him and it's pointless.

He called me last night and we talked for, like, two minutes, and he told me to text him today. I did, and he didn't really hold up the conversation. So I'm not going to initiate anything anymore with him, because it's useless and I just feel dumb in the end.

Lewiston was great. I went to school with Camila. I went to her yearbook class, and then to her friend Weston's government class with him. Weston is Camila's good friend whose style is alternative and who looks kind of Asian. He is so cool! One of the most poetic and serious people I have ever met, but crazy and reckless and happy and darkly sad and an incredibly spiritual, creative soul. His life is a monument to anything strange, beautiful, and fucked up. I can't even describe him accurately, holy shit.

In Weston's class the teacher didn't even care that I was there.

He asked me where my paperwork was after Weston jokingly but half-seriously told him I was a new student. I said I didn't have any, and then awkwardly sat down. That would never be okay at my high school! You would have to check in at the front office and get a visitor's pass, at least, if they even let you bring a relative or friend to school.

We ate lunch in Weston's orange VW bus, it was fabulous. I met a couple more of his and Camila's friends who were very nice and cool. They are different from the people in Boise. It's like they are more accepting and not judgmental. They are exciting in this creative, carefree way. I get the most alluring vibes from them, like they are real and true. We also hung out with Joel for a while. He's cool, the stoner with shaggy hair that I met before at one of their parties. And he's cute and nice and likes good music. I'm in love.

Camila and I ate at a pizza place for dinner with Maddie, who is Camila's older sister, Maddie's boyfriend who is really tall and fat and has super curly, brown hair, Grandma, Camila's dad, Sawyer, and Mom, and it was delicious.

Joel sent Camila a text that said, "Ana's so cute, hook a brotha up," so I felt good about myself, and I love him. But there was no time to hang out with him again because we were doing stuff with our family after dinner, and then I had to leave for home early the next morning.

Anyway, I'm home now already.

26 March 2009

I'm drunk. This is what I yearn for: Conrad, inside jokes, someone truthful, waking up next to, owning, belonging to, BEING, "Stay or Leave" by Dave Matthews Band, someone to love me for real, truth, truth, truth, remember stories, all the days I'll exist, I want to exist with someone I know is perfect, drugs don't have to be involved,

he'll be fucked up and we'll laugh and unity. Makes me feel important and alive and real. Not Conrad or Eli. Quiet and sensitive and smart and funny. I feel so important. Unreal, but I'm a tiny unit, insignificant, why can't I be all that I want? Poems, books, coffee, driving, music. It's simple yet complicated. UNDERSTANDING, love.

28 March 2009

Today we had a soccer game and my coach told me that I need to play myself out of this funk I've been in all spring season. Shit. I know I've been playing bad, but I thought it was only a weird phase. Now I feel like it'll never pass and I'll play like shit in college. It's making me nervous and worried. I seriously pass the ball to the other team, like, every time I get it, and I'm so worried.

I have nothing to live for, no passion, no direction in life. I have no idea what I want to do after college, what kind of job I want. It's scary and frustrating. The more I think about it, the more I feel like I don't want to do anything. I just want to sit around and read and wear weird outfits and, I dunno, be famous or something. Be able to skydive and do other fun shit. I don't want to work, I just want to travel and play.

Sometimes I want to write. Most of all I want to be a gunslinger. I want to feel things. I want crazy shit to happen to me. I want random phenomena to determine the direction of my life. I want spontaneity to decide who I am and what I do. I want to meet someone with big plans, legitimate plans, someone who'll take me on adventures.

I want to be part of something important, something fantastic, but it should spring upon me when I'm not looking. It'll happen because I was in the exact right place at the exact right time. This is what I hope for but I fear these situations only happen in the movies. I'm worried. I worry way too much and think way too far ahead.

03 April 2009

I got my hair cut by Jenna. She did such an incredible job, she really is good at cutting hair. It makes me happy that she is doing something she loves and is successful at.

05 April 2009

Yesterday my family was gone skiing (I didn't want to go) so I watched *28 Days Later* and took a nap and memorized the rest of my presentation for my senior project. It was relaxing.

Spring is here! Today is warm. Sawyer and Dad are working on Sawyer's car in the garage. I went out there and practiced my speech while walking down the sidewalk. I present officially on the 14th or 15th. It's going to be the best feeling in the world when I get that done with. The feeling is called "freedom." It's a fabulous thing if you've never felt it.

And it's mixed with summer and carefree and warmth and barely any homework until actual summer when school ends, and the knowledge that I won't ever have to go back to the shit-hole called high school, or see the people at high school ever again! In my whole life!

07 April 2009

Today I saw *Slumdog Millionaire* at the dollar theatre with Sawyer and Lacy because it's Dollar Tuesday! Incredible that so many terrible things happen to people all the time and they just pull through it, keep living because they have to. They had a stupendous soundtrack as well, like M.I.A. She's super interesting. I wish I could be that interesting.

Lately, it's weird, I feel like being famous is the only thing worth doing in life, because it means that you've accomplished something, or that you're the best at something.* I feel like those are the only things that matter. Or at least being important. I don't feel that important. I'm only one person of billions. That's so minuscule that my brain isn't complex enough to comprehend it.

I don't feel that special or interesting. These things have been bothering me lately. I dunno why. I want to be the people I meet in books and movies.

[*Ana: Being really famous would suck balls. For you, at least. Like, imagine not being able to leave your house without people following you around and filming and taking pictures of you and criticizing your every move. You could never wander around new cities anonymously, sit alone in cafés, go out in public without everyone staring and trying to talk to you. It would be awful!

You can most definitely accomplish something and be "important" and be proud of your life without being famous. And actually, you probably could be a little famous in a particular niche and not be recognized everywhere you go, but being super famous like certain actors and musicians would not be as awesome as everyone thinks it would be. –J.]

11 April 2009

Today I played my old team, which was awkward. I play for a different team now because they are way better, and I felt like in order for me to get better I needed to play on a team that would challenge me more. I also did ODP with most of the girls on the better team before I switched to them, and their coach is one of the ODP coaches, so I pretty much knew everybody anyway. ODP stands for Olympic Development Program, which is just another soccer thing, but we get to travel a lot and play teams from everywhere. Another fun thing to do!

Anyway, we beat my old team by like 6-0, or something. I didn't score. After that I came home and read Sawyer's huge book about Buddhism.

14 April 2009

Today I presented my senior project! It wasn't bad; my panel was nice and asked easy questions. Today was better than good, only because I got that over with. Soccer was good, too, and then Lacy and Sawyer and I went to *Paul Blart: Mall Cop* at the dollar theatre. It was funny and dumb. We drank during it. I'm a little tipsy so it's cool.

I was thinking about time and how I'm already done with senior project, and almost done with high school. I think back to certain times when I thought about this moment I'm in right now, and what it'd be like, and now I'm living it.

What I imagined is often so different from what actually ends up happening. It's crazy to me! Like, right now I have no idea what college will be like, or if I will meet someone really important to me, or if I'll get a job, or what I'll be doing after college. But soon I will know all these things, and I'll think back to this moment and say, "Wow, I'm already doing what I imagined," or "I never thought my life would be like this," or I dunno, whatever!

15 April 2009

Night. There's something in the way the trees sway under the streetlamps. Drunkenly. Influenced by that orangeish intoxicating luminescence. In a secret language they suggest life's meaning as tiny particles floating in the air. As something whisper-like, nudging you gently, playing with your hair when you feel someone watching you.

The buzz of caffeine in the bloodstream. When you drive home through the swell of night's ripest flesh, that black, deep desire of the sun's absence, you see the trees dancing with the streetlamps, and you wish you were in on that secret they keep.

17 April 2009

Last night before I fell asleep I was thinking about how good I feel when it rains, and how things always look much more vibrant when they're glistening and the sky is that blue-gray that's so beautiful. Then I thought about gardens and how luscious they are when everything's blooming and the grass is bright, and how great it'd be if you could lose yourself in a garden huge and vast.

I always think of this desktop picture on our computer that is of this giant castle in the distance, and all that's in front of it to where the photographer is standing is only grass. An evenly cut, glowing plane, widespread and perfect.

I'm just bored, there's no adventure save the books I read. People are selfish and judgmental. I always say the wrong things. In the movies people always say the right things, and their traumas are justified somehow. But in real life, things don't happen like that. Maybe they do, actually, it's just hard for me to feel it. Maybe I don't feel that way about my life because I know myself fully.

Other people often seem mysterious and interesting, but most of the time they turn out to be awful. Maybe I am mysterious and interesting but I don't know because I'm too immersed in myself. Self-absorbed.

18 April 2009

I went to the hot springs with Sawyer and Lacy. It took about an hour to get there, and you have to hike up this trail that seemed dangerous for drunkards. When we found the trail it was already dark, and we saw some naked people, which was gross and funny. I also saw this girl that was on my soccer team a while ago that no one liked, it was weird. I'm not really sure why no one liked her. I didn't have a problem with her. I think the other girls on my team are just bitchy, haha.

There were three pools, so we went to the one highest up and we had it to ourselves because the people there were leaving. We drank malt liquor and talked about random stuff. Later a whole ton of people came, and they shared their alcohol and glow-sticks with us. There were a billion stars. It was beautiful and peaceful until all those people came.

We eventually left around two in the morning. We were drunk walking down the hill, a bit treacherous but we are risk-takers. Fearlessness brought on by intoxicants.

We went to this restaurant that never closes. It was around three in the morning and totally packed with people! I got hash browns, eggs, bacon, and toast. I had some of Sawyer's crepe, which was fucking good! All for five dollars, holy shit.

Then we got home at around four and I went to bed. Sawyer went back to Lacy's; he's still there, I think.

When I was drunk last night, on the drive back, I realized how young I really am, and how before I know it I'll be old and wrinkly and worn out. But for now I have a strong body and I'm healthy,* and in that moment I thought that was so profound and interesting. It is still a weighty truth, but the permanence of it then seemed much more vast.

[*Ana: You could be healthier if you stopped eating death and suffering. Research veganism. You'll find it fits perfectly with your perception of morality (you know, the whole "treat others as you'd like to be treated" thing), spirituality (you know, that there are actually no "others"), and ideals regarding integrity. Quit eating animal products and your love handles you hate intensely will melt away. Plus, maybe you'll start to notice sooner how all life is sacred, how everything is connected. –J.]

I love hanging out with Sawyer and Lacy because I don't feel like the third wheel. It's because I have a family tie; Sawyer and I are siblings so we're important to each other. I know that he cares about me, not like people at school who I know don't give a shit. Even people that are my good friends, like Lisbet and Eli. I don't think they care as much as they could anymore.

I don't know, life is so complicated. That's why I want to become enlightened,* so I can fully experience the depth of life's complexity. Becoming fully aware seems pretty great. More than great.

[*Ana: You NEED to start meditating. It's the only way. I mean, look at all those celestial bodies in your 12th house! If that isn't an obvious indication, I don't know what is. –J.]

21 April 2009

Yesterday was 4/20 and I didn't smoke because I couldn't get any mota. But I went on a bike ride with Sawyer and Lacy, and we played frisbee golf at the park, and ate at a restaurant downtown, and rode to this new ice cream place where you serve yourself.

It was warm and we rode on the greenbelt, and the breeze on my face and through my hair made everything surreal. I remember thinking that if I could just stay in that moment forever, or at least a little longer, I'd be perfectly content.

I feel like time's sneaking away from me, softly. I feel like when I'm doing something fun it passes too quickly. Before I know it, it's over.

22 April 2009

Today Davis got me out of fitness class since he's in Newspaper and can call people out of class, and we played the championship backgammon game in the school library. And I totally won! So I'm the best ever, basically. We've been competing and decided that today would be the final battle.

Before lunch our whole senior class took the '09 picture. Exactly one month before school's out and I never have to see this hellhole ever again.

Soccer was okay today. We ran five 90-yard sprints, it really wasn't that hard.

25 April 2009

Today's Saturday! I had one soccer game against a team a

year younger than us. I scored four times, haha. It was fun, kind of. I just felt tired during it.

I finished watching *Charlie Bartlett*, and it made me feel so happy and sad and left out and in love and hopeful and wishful and not alone and mad and unlucky and like I don't belong here. He was funny, nice, sincere, and real, and I wish I could be that way, you know?

I wish I could talk to people and make friends with such ease and have something meaningful to say and at the right moments, or something witty or funny. I wish I wasn't awkward and I wish everyone was friends. I wish when I saw someone with something weird or crazy or different I could say something charming about it, but teasing at the same time.

02 May 2009

I finished reading *The Road* for English and it was okay. I dunno, I didn't really like it that much. Everybody in my class was like, "OH MY GOD, *The Road* is the best book ever!" And I thought it was kind of boring. Actually, not kind of. Super boring. Like how many times can you describe how gray and ashy everything is?

I saw this girl's Lookbook profile today (Lookbook is this fashion website that Weston showed me) and all her clothes were so cool and bohemian/comfortable/grunge, and I felt jealous because that's what I want to be like and how I want to dress. I got super depressed because sometimes I don't like who I am and it frustrates me.

And then I see people who completely encompass all that I wish I was, who have this subtle essence of having figured everything out, and I get intensely jealous. It's like they're part of this secret club where all the eccentric and interesting people hang out and talk about how cool they are, and I'm always left on the outside wishing to be included.

Everything's strange. Why do people do things? And I am a person in this moment, lucky me, it's my turn. The people I know, what I spend my time doing, it's all so random. What isn't random?

I want to live forever, baby.

I love those dreams where you're running for a long time and you feel light and airy, as if you could keep running for all eternity and never stop. It's beautiful to experience. It's like the epitome of freedom for me. Also, flying dreams. I had one the other night, it was relaxing.

People don't care. Only about themselves.

05 May 2009

Cinco de Mayo. Woo. Today sucked. I tried to sell Lacy's old clothes at a couple of used fashion stores, and neither store wanted anything. So I drove all the way downtown and around and came up fruitless. What a waste. And I kept making wrong turns, like in the parking garage I almost went in the "Do Not Enter" way, and I was so embarrassed!

I took a nap when I finally got home, and I don't even know if I fell asleep at all, I just laid there for, like, two hours. When I finally got up, I had this strange and deep feeling of despair, it was really perturbing. I just sat there not knowing what to do with myself and feeling dreadful. It was bizarre.

08 May 2009

Friday. I've been too confused about myself lately. I should quit analyzing. I took the AP English test, it was all right. My essays were shit, nothing unsuspected there.

I had a women's league game at six today. Just another random soccer thing with women of all ages. We won by a lot. I scored three goals but it was awful regardless. I played terribly. Tomorrow I have a game at two.

Ten days of school left, is that unbelievable? I know. I'm so relieved to be getting out of this shithole. I feel desensitized. I don't feel things anymore. And I don't even know if that is true. I just really hate school, and I'm barely able to drag myself through it.

Beneath the perspective veiling truth is a thin layer of anxiousness. Horrible isolation revealing unity's non-existence, brought about by certain, creeping substances. I'm always frightened. Who am I? I'm supposed to be productive, punctual. Why, why, why? Why anything? Importance isn't real. No connections anywhere. What am I to do without reason? Shifting monsters reach for me, lost in reality's subjectiveness. Ominous feelings of unease.

10 May 2009

Yesterday Sawyer and I went to the dollar theatre to see *Gran Torino* and got drunk during it. It was fun because that movie is hilarious! Clint Eastwood is extremely racist in it, it's ridiculous. Everyone in the movie just puts up with his shit. He's so awful that it makes you laugh. Obviously racism isn't a hilarious topic, but that movie put a weird spin on it that was somehow funny.

When we got back home we played backgammon and took two shots of Black Absinthe and got super hammered. At least I was. We walked to the elementary school by our house and took pictures of us holding sparklers. We laid down in the middle of the intersection by our house. Exhilarating.

Oh, and I'm pretty sure I peed in the middle of the road in our neighborhood. When I woke up this morning I had intense spins, it was terrible and nauseating. I dozed in bed till I was starving, then got up, ate a little cereal, felt sick, and went back to bed. I told Mom I was still tired. When I got up for the second time I felt better but still spinny.

17 May 2009

One week of school left. Today's Sunday and Sawyer, Grandma, and I drove back from Lewiston. Sawyer and I drove up on Friday, and on Friday and Saturday night Camila and I drank with Weston.

Saturday was his high school graduation party, and there were lots of people and food and alcohol. We stayed the night there because Camila's parents were gone so we didn't have to be home. It was fun. All their friends are nice and funny and they listen to such good music! I knew a lot of bands they had and got some new ones to look up.

Joel, who I have a secret crush on, told Camila that I was so fine, and that made me feel happy. He and I talked a lot on Saturday when we were drunk, but he never kissed me! He never even made an attempt! I can't stop thinking about how weird that was, because guys always try to kiss you, especially when they're drunk. So usually I don't have to do anything and they just make a move.

It makes me mad because I totally wanted to make out with him.* We smoked mota in his car alone, too.

125

[*Ana: Use your initiative! You make the move! What are you afraid of? You already knew he is into you. –J.]

That night I slept in Weston's bed with him. We stayed up till three talking and listening to music on his laptop. It was weird because he's a sad drunk. Like, he was talking about how this girl at the party asked him if he was gay, and he's not so it made him feel really bad.

He talked about how I couldn't understand his feelings, and how people don't care about him, and that's all false! So many people love him, and I started to get depressed because people only care about themselves, and we're all alone and there's nothing to do about that.

It's weird though, because Weston thinks that I can't understand how he feels, but I feel the same way about many things. I have no friends compared to Camila and them, and they're all so happy and cool and I wish I could have something like that, and be social. Then when I say these things I feel like I'm just one of those people that only care about themselves because I'm just focusing on myself and my experiences.

I never tell anyone these things. My feelings are like catch-22's, and I hate myself so much sometimes, and I don't think I should, or else I should think of these feelings as beautiful in a way, because they are.

I don't know what I want in life. Maybe it's friends that won't betray me, maybe it's love, maybe it's enlightenment, maybe it's fame. But often I think that whatever a person has, we all end up feeling the same as before we had it.

18 May 2009

Today was just another day. School sucked, only four days left of high school. FOREVER! God, I can't stop thinking about what Camila and Weston and Joel are doing. Right now, as I write this, I wonder what they are all thinking about or doing.

Last night I downloaded a ton of music that I got from them, and I keep thinking about how they love the songs I'm listening to, how so many people have loved the songs I've loved. And how I first thought about that last part because it was in *The Perks of Being a Wallflower*. I can relate to the kid in there because I guess I don't have that many friends that I truly care about and want to be around.

It was nice to spend time with people that are like me. I mean, I do have friends I care about, but not many that are like me and that I hang out with a lot. I dunno, it's weird. I'm excited for college. Hopefully I'll make friends, and I really want to be genuine and be taken seriously. I hope that works out.

20 May 2009

Two days left of my high school career. I'm almost a real person!

26 May 2009

So much has happened to me these last few days! First of all, I'm done with high school. For forever. High school was the worst thing that ever happened to me, so to get that done with is mind-blowingly pleasant.

On the last day we had three assemblies, all about not drinking and driving and shit like that, ruining my good mood. We also had the senior slideshow, which was dumb.

Most of the pictures were either of Isaac because he put it together, or of annoying girls with too much makeup that submitted a trillion pictures of themselves.

Isaac is this skinny punk-ish red-haired kid with huge dreads and he always seems to have boogers in his nose. He always wants to talk to River and I because we are weird and cool, but we don't like him that much so we try to avoid him. We call him "the dreaded ginge."

We got our yearbooks and then went to the senior picnic thing at the park downtown. Lisbet, Eli, and I got super high at Eli's new house downtown out of a bong before going to the picnic. I just freak out whenever I get high because I go to a bad place and things feel evil and ominous and I don't like it. So that's how it felt, and the whole time Davis and I played backgammon.

I lost Lisbet and Eli, got really anxious, and didn't focus on anything Davis was saying, although I still beat him at backgammon. I also signed a few people's yearbooks, but I forgot mine in the car because I was too high so I didn't get anyone else's signatures. So that was cool.

After that whole experience we drove to Pocatello for the state soccer tournament, which we won. It was cool, I scored some goals. Then last night my soccer team had a party and we all got super drunk and it was hilarious.

This morning I had to get up at 8:30 for graduation practice. I got four hours of sleep total. Then I had my real graduation tonight, which I got home from an hour and a half ago. It was long and boring and it put me in a terrible mood because all the shit we had to wear made it very hot and uncomfortable. But I'm okay now.

I didn't go to our fucking party after graduation, but I don't care. I'm tired and I hate all those stupid people anyway. Grandma gave me $100, my parents bought an ice cream cake, it's officially summer, and I never have to be in high school ever again. Boy, am I excited!

27 May 2009

Sawyer froze some bees that he caught, so we put them on leashes made of thread. But I think he killed them by leaving them in the freezer for too long because they never woke up after we took them out. I was disappointed because I really wanted to fly my bee around the neighborhood.*

[*Ana: Y'all are terrorists. –J.]

29 May 2009

Today I donated plasma with Sawyer! It was crazy, I love doing new things. They almost wouldn't let me because I take Amoxicillin* for my acne and you can't give plasma if you take that for anything except acne. At first they didn't ask what it was for, but they realized this and then let me give after they figured it out.

[*Ana: This will destroy your gut bacteria and consequently your mental health. Not advised. –J.]

It was weird because all the people giving looked like creepers so I was scared kind of, but then once I got into the actual room they do it in, everything looked professional and nice and not white-trash, like how the waiting room and the outside of the building and most of the people looked.

I made $25 today, and the next time I go in I'll make $35. You can only go twice a week, with at least a day in between. They also have movies playing constantly for the people giving plasma to watch. Today I watched *Quantum of Solace* while the needle was in me. It's like getting paid to watch a movie.

After it was over I felt kind of weird, like I couldn't create very good sentences. It's like that when I get high, except when I'm high it's way worse. I think it is neat to do weird things like this. It's random and I love random.

30 May 2009

Usually when summer comes I want it to never end, but I decided today that from here on out I am actually a real person, kind of. So from now on this is life, and I get to do fun things and live in Seattle and be friendly and smile at people when we make eye contact, and learn interesting things and live on my own.

So, actually, I don't care if summer ends and I have to go to school, because college is going to be exciting and adventurous and spectacular and frightening and illicit and secretive and open-minded and liberating, and the time of my fucking life. It might even be better than summer. You never know.

02 June 2009

Today it rained, which was like when you cry because you know everything is okay and that you are safe. The temperature was perfect, not too cold. I got up around 9:30 a.m. and went to breakfast with Sawyer and Lacy. It was funny, our waitress ate some Pez candies we offered her, and we left three more on her tip and then spied on her outside to see if she would eat them. She did!

I gave plasma for the second time and they gave me $35! It's great, it's like getting paid to watch movies or read a book. I watched *The Core*, but it was dumb.

I also had soccer today, and I think I am able to truthfully say that it was the hardest practice of my life. We did a million sprints, in groups of four people. It may have been really hard because I gave plasma like an hour before working out. I dunno if that's such a good idea.

07 June 2009

Melancholy pervades my insignificant entity. We went to Lewiston for Camila's graduation party. It was last night, and I got drunk with Weston, Joel, and Alex, and Camila sort of, but she had to socialize and was beating everybody at beer pong. Everything went by too fast; it was like it didn't happen. We took shots outside the huge shed/garage thing where the party was when the adults weren't looking. It was secret and hidden and rebellious.

We played Nintendo a lot, and I played beer pong once, which I did well in, strangely enough. It was weird because I usually suck at beer pong since I never play, since I don't like beer. Oh! We also performed a real and intense Underwear Club meeting, it was so much fucking fun! When we were little Maddie, Camila, and I ran around in our underwear and quoted *Dexter's Laboratory* and were members of the Underwear Club.

This time we ran down Camila's street in our underwear and it was pitch dark. We ran from Weston's VW bus, which we also smoked mota in and talked about Sasquatch, this music festival they went to. I didn't get to go but I'd like to next year.

We listened to the crickets. They were loud and brilliant, as if they were trying to stop time and keep us in that precious moment for all eternity so we could share it for always. Weston said they were trying to tell him something. I think he was right. Everything was surreal, something I'm new to, something I cherish. When you have something to say they listen and can relate.

God, I wish I could remember all the things perfectly, but I always forget inside jokes and what I ate for breakfast yesterday and what I'm thinking when I'm drunk or high. It infuriates me! It's 9:30 p.m. and still light out. Raining. Lately I've just been sad. Maybe it's loneliness? I feel left out of things and like no one cares about me, but I know they do. I feel like I'm going crazy inside my mind.

I hate how when you're drunk you have a lot of fun with someone, and the next time you see them you're sober and it's awkward. I hate that! I hate being awkward with people but I so am. I never know what to say, it's awful. I hate how different levels of perception can prohibit you from connecting with someone who isn't on the same level.

I wish I'd think the same things normally as I would when I'm drunk or high. Actually, I think at least when I'm drunk I think the same things. Maybe when I'm high, too, it's just I feel worried and anxious when I'm high, and paranoid. I communicate things wrong as well. When I'm drunk I'm not afraid to tell people what I think, which is such a good feeling.

I'm trapped in my mind and there's no way out.

19 June 2009

The past few days I've been at regionals in Lancaster, California. Our hotel was in Hesperia, an hour away from the fields. I roomed with three other girls on my team. We played Hawaii and lost 2-1. I scored and we totally could have won. We tied Arizona 1-1 and I played awful. We beat Washington 2-1 and I scored once. We didn't get to go on to the finals, though. It was lame.

On our last night we stole a bottle of wine from our coach's room while we were asking him to buy us alcohol, which he didn't, and one of the girls on my team opened it with a ball pump and a pen. It was awesome. So we got a bottle of wine in celebration, but that was it. Not enough to get drunk.

I flew back yesterday, spent all day traveling, and I read a lot on the plane rides.

21 June 2009

I always try to think about myself like how I think about people in the movies, or just people that I think are cool, like Weston or Lisbet's sister. But I can't, because in the movies or books or songs there's always something to say about those people.

Like in this Red Hot Chili Peppers song called "She's Only 18." When I hear the lyrics I feel like this girl is being explained in a definitive way; we all can feel her vibe! I wish that I could hear someone sing about me, say a few lines about me, so I'd know who I am, what my vibe is, and be able to think about myself as being interesting or mysterious. So that I'd like myself, in a sense.

That is what goes on in my head. It's fucking weird and complicated and one of the reasons I think I'm crazy.

One time when Eli, Lisbet, and I were high, I asked Eli to tell me about myself because I thought it'd make me feel a little less insane, because I feel *really* insane when I'm high and I hate it. But instead, he just changed the subject and started talking to Lisbet, and I felt like such an idiot. It was weird. Especially because I was high. It was worse than…I dunno, anything.

I feel like feeling this way about myself, the way I feel towards people in movies and books and songs, is extremely important and I don't know why. I feel like real life should be how it is in the movies (obviously not all movies, but a lot of them) and I can't figure out if it is or isn't!*

[*Ana: It is; you only need to get out of Boise and go to a huge, multicultural city. –J.]

I wish I could be older so that things could happen to me because right now nothing happens. I feel like I'm going insane thinking about feelings and vibes all the time. Maybe I am a real person who's bothered by the complexity of existence and the way I am and the way I think.

I'm nervous for college. And real life. Because I still feel like a little kid sometimes. And I feel immature a lot of the time, too, or either more mature than everyone else. It's weird. It's making me insane because I feel like I've never been a real person before. Now I'm about to be real, and it's fucking weird and difficult. I feel like I won't be able to do things on my own, like taxes and dealing with loans and finances and shit like that.* I'm just worried.

[*Ana: You don't have to know about all of this right now, but educating yourself about personal finance is imperative. The sooner you do this, the better. They also don't really teach this in school, at least high school, so take initiative and investigate on your own. –J.]

Earth, fire, wood, and burning things, and living and dying, and what is living and dying? And all that we know is stored inside our tiny brains. But only if we could use our entire minds, we could control everything around us, we could be who we want to be. Insane, everything's so insane all the time. Plants, people. Aren't we all a little bit insane?

I wish things were like the movies, how sometimes you just know what's right and what you should do in a certain situation. Problems with friends are solved, if you have friends, that is. I wish I wasn't extremely goddamn awkward around people. It's a hindrance to living in society.

I wish I could find someone like me. Someone who feels the same. Maybe I don't want that. Maybe I want someone completely different, and I don't mean a boyfriend. Just a friend. I wish I could say that I had a best friend. I wish that we would do all the things together, and be nice to people and wear funny clothes and listen to the same music and both want to do something adventurous when we're older. But we'd find adventures on our own, here. Or in seattle. Or wherever we end up meeting.

I feel like this life sucks, and that I could be doing something much better if I weren't trapped in this bullshit city without friends. Like, in Lewiston, Camila always has these great stories to tell me about her and Weston and all their friends and all the crazy shit they do. And they are fun, they aren't like here. I know I don't want to live in Lewiston, but it feels like the people my age there are way friendlier and better than in Boise.

Why can't people be childish? And immature? It's all I want: to meet someone who wants to do crazy shit without drugs or alcohol. Because it's weird and they're weird and exciting and mysterious and fun and who I want to be. I want to find someone I can look up to and follow around and watch and love.

I want someone to care about me. Lisbet never cared about me, but there was no one else so I stuck with her. Is it this state? Everyone in Idaho just seems fucking weird to me. Like really conservative, or Mormon, or both, or with a mindset that you shouldn't do certain things, and I think you should do everything. Even if sometimes it's bad.

You can do bad things with people you love because it makes it all right. To a point, I mean. Like, you probably shouldn't do heroin with people you love because it'll fuck you both up. But I mean, like, shrooms and weed and getting drunk. It's okay with people that care about you. In moderation, of course.

What was I going to mention? I always wonder what it would be like to go crazy after being alone for too long. Like in *Castaway*, when he talks to the volleyball. Would you think after a while, "I'm talking to an inanimate object. This is happening because I've been alone for so long. My mind is deteriorating." Could you think rationally about the subject of your insanity? I dunno, it's weird.

Sometimes I think that's what's happening to me. Every day I'm alone, and I sit in my house and wonder what I'm going to do with my fucking life because everything sounds like shit and I don't want to talk to the people that I know, and it sucks. And I want to be somebody badly.

Like Angelina Jolie. She's amazing and she's doing things that are fun. She has Brad Pitt to talk to and they seem so in love and they care about each other, and that's what I want to be doing. Especially when everybody looks at you and knows who you are and are jealous of you. Like me being jealous.

I always think of Kurt Cobain and Courtney Love. I think being involved with someone that's in a band would be cool, because you're behind the scenes of something everyone loves, and you're important because you're a part of it, even if you're not in the band. You spend time with someone that everybody wishes they could be spending time with. And you could be exclusive with them.

Everyone would want to know what you two talk about when you're alone, but only you'd know. It's alluring to me, that mysteriousness and intimacy of relationships between famous people. That's how other people would think of it as: mysterious.

23 June 2009

Today was the second day of my summer workout packet for college soccer. My college team gets these packets over the summer so that we can be in shape by the time we start preseason. It took about three hours to complete today, which was fucking irritating! Yesterday's only took about an hour, but today's was much longer, and I had to drive to my high school to use their soccer field, which isn't even marked out, so I had to guess on the length of it.

Yesterday I gave plasma. The guy that gave me my money at the end was cute and he asked me what I was reading. When I told him I'm reading Stephen King's *Dark Tower* series he said Stephen King is his favorite author. It made me happy because he was such a real person to me and it was comforting. Because so often I interact with people that don't seem real. Like the lights are on but nobody's home. You know?

28 June 2009

I'm back from freshman orientation in Seattle! We stayed in Bellevue in a nice hotel that was surprisingly inexpensive. It took about seven and a half hours to drive there. The next day was orientation and it wasn't as terrible as I thought it was going to be. Everyone in my group was really nice and it wasn't that hard to meet new people.

I registered for classes, and my classes will be on Mondays, Wednesdays, and Fridays. I have no class earlier than 9:30 a.m.! I'm going to take a class about Japanese pop culture that is like an introduction to college class for freshmen, an Introduction to Logic class, and a class about the Middle Ages.

After that was all over we went to Fremont and Ballard and to the beach in Ballard. Quaint little shops, beautiful scenery, sun and sand. Everything is green and blooming. I am super excited to live there!

04 July 2009

It's Independence Day! Today Mom and I drove back from Lewiston, where we've been all week and the reason I haven't been writing. I had a lot of fun. Camila and I slept at Weston's house with his dogs in his parents' bed because he is in Europe with his family and we were housesitting for them.

The wiener dog named Scout slept in the bed with us, which was weird, and Murphy, the huge fat Rottweiler, smelled terrible and slept next to the bed on the floor. Weston's house was dirty, but that's okay because it was fun anyway.

I did my college workouts all week. Camila and I hung out with some of her friends in their pool, and with her boyfriend, Bob, and stoner Joel. We drank alcohol.

I drank out of Joel's mom's mug that says, "You are special today" on it. You are special today, but only today. Another funny thing: "Fish, sh, sh!" Because we ate fish that night and that's how I said it when we told Bob what we had for dinner, and then I cracked up and had to go outside to get some air because I couldn't stop laughing. I guess it was only funny if you were there, haha.

Now I'm sitting on the roof of my house in the dark watching the fireworks, explosions of color bursting every few seconds and in all directions. I feel like there is a raging war all around me, but I'm escaping it for the time being in my secret hideout. Perched on the roof I am the surveyor of all action and demise.

It's like being a part of something meaningful, but behind the scenes. Everything surrounds me but I have no responsibility, no duty, only to wait and watch and hide and be silent. To sneak and think. I love that feeling.

11 July 2009

New hair by Jenna! I love it. Short and bleached blonde and asymmetrical.

14 July 2009

I have just been witness to perhaps one of the most moving, fascinating, and delightful movies in creation. In short, it was bloody brilliant! *Harry Potter and the Half-blood Prince*. I was transfixed throughout the entire movie. When it was over I was left with this deep feeling of longing and melancholia, because what was held before me, tauntingly out of reach, is not real and something I can never be a part of. Admitting this makes me want to have a temper tantrum.

Why can't I be a part of something so cherished and important? Why can't there be clever, fun, intelligent, and kind people as my best friends? Why can't I have friends that'll never betray me, and let me cry on their shoulders when one of them does? Why can't I be vulnerable with a wise wizard who helps me up and guides me? Why can't I be faced with a terrible task, an even more difficult decision? Why do I always want what I can't have?

The warm embrace of castle corridors, stones thick in their ancient gray skin, hovering like a mother holding a child. Comforting like a secret hiding place. These things aren't real to me and I can never have what I want so badly. These are my vulnerable thoughts and I hope if anyone ever reads this they'll understand my secret heart.

And how maybe in my heart, I've always wanted a best friend, someone I can absolutely rely on, always, someone like me, someone who cares about me. Harry, Ron, and Hermione have that and it's unfair. To have a trio of best friends. For a girl to have two guy best friends and have it not be weird.

I feel a lot like Harry sometimes, but I suppose we all do, don't we? Which I loathe because I'm selfish and I want it all to myself because I feel like no one understands. I watch these movies and I see how life's supposed to be, and then I walk outside the theatre and all I see are the girls with their caked makeup faces and their boyfriends who don't give a shit about anything but sex, and nobody cares about the things that matter, and nobody cares about each other.

We all pretend but all we truly care about are material items and ourselves.

All the time I wish I didn't need to watch movies to lose

myself in. I wish I *was* part of that certain movie. I hate that I'm only another fan. Sometimes I feel very important, or more special than others, and I know that's a naive and proud and ridiculous feeling, but I still feel it. I feel like I have something to do, a purpose, but I don't know what it is.

Then other days I feel low and like just another face. Then other days I have no idea how I feel at all, or who I am, or what I'm doing.

19 July 2009

Today we drove home from Mary's house. She's my great aunt and lives a couple hours north of Lewiston. Seven-hour drive. We went to Silverwood, this amusement park that's really close to her house, with Maddie and Camila, and Trae and Lily, my second cousins that I don't know that well since we never see each other.

It was an incredible experience. So much has happened, I dunno where to start. I suppose I'll ramble for a while.

We went to Silverwood twice. The first time just Maddie, Camila, Trae, Lily, and I. Then the next day everybody went. And Mom rode the big coaster, Tremors! She is such a baby and doesn't want to ride them ever. I adore Tremors. I think I could ride it 50 times in a row and not get bored of it. Roller coasters are my fucking favorite things in the world.

After Silverwood, on the way back to Mary's house, I saw a shooting star. We had to stop for two trains and Maddie yelled at us for wanting to get out of the car to watch them because she thought it was dangerous. Camila screamed loudly when we slammed on the brakes for the second train because Maddie almost didn't stop on accident.

Maddie also shut my fingers in the window. It hurt like hell and I started yelling and couldn't stop until she realized what she had done and rolled the window down. Camila punched her really hard as punishment for hurting me. It was funny how weirdly protective she got.

We made s'mores and hot dogs with a campfire in Mary's backyard, and drank coffee in the morning. Their dogs are blue heelers, furry and fuzzy and speckled. One of them destroyed my perfect balls of hemp that I use for bracelets. Now I have a multicolored hairball to disentangle. Oh, well.

Camila and I hung out with Weston for a night. We had a midnight picnic in the middle of a random field. Today Mom and I drove all the way home. On Tuesday Camila and Weston are going to drive down here to visit me.

24 July 2009

Today's Friday. Camila and Weston are already gone; they left today at about noon. Weston let me keep his underwear, is that weird? They are comfortable, I'm wearing them now.

We went downtown shopping, and I sold some clothes at a recycled fashion store, and we stopped by Alive After Five, this live music thing every Wednesday by the circle fountain. We also went to Goodwill and Savers and I got some black slip-on sneakers that are awesome, and we got three mugs that all look alike.

That night we got drunk with the wine Weston brought, except Camila fell asleep early. Weston and I walked to the elementary school by my house. We took pictures of him next to the sign because he was wearing his Chief Joseph shirt he bought from Urban Outfitters, and the elementary school's emblem has Chief Joseph in it.

We all slept on the futon outside on the patio. Weston kissed me. It was weird; I'm strangely attracted to him.

One thing that's weird and it sucked was that Camila would have moments where she was really rude to me. Like, she'd make snippy little retorts to things I'd say, or make fun of me or what's in my room, like my Hello Kitty stuff. And I think it was only because Weston was there, because she's never acted like that. I think subconsciously she was establishing Weston as her territory and that I, in no way, was to be better than her…funnier, prettier, whatever.

I'm not saying that I am better than her in any way, because I don't think I am, and in reality I have always thought that she is super pretty, and way prettier than me. I'm just saying I think she felt subtly threatened by me. It was as if she was saying that she's the alpha, the one in charge. But she isn't attracted to Weston, so I dunno why she was acting like that. She also has a boyfriend!

It was strange and disheartening, because the worst thing ever is to be put down by people you love, people you consider very close to you. People you've shared your secrets with and who you're vulnerable with. It really sucked for a while. It eventually got way better though, and today they left so I'm feeling a bit sad.

28 July 2009

I went camping with my parents. We went fishing when we got there around six or seven in the morning, but we had no luck. I took a nap in the car and that's when Dad started catching fish. We rode our bikes to find a campground and we found one that was hidden with lots of shade. We ate hot dogs and I read a lot.

That night around midnight we went out to the dock on the lake and looked out over the water. It was breathtaking. Every star was visible, and we could see the Milky Way Galaxy. The water was smooth and still and deep and the stars were caught in its blackness. The trees and mountains across the lake were bulky shadows, also reflected in the water.

I think I could've stayed in that moment forever, but it all slipped away through my fingers. Like the water created by my mind's waves, unable to be hidden away in my secret boxes. I know that the moment I'm capturing right now, on paper, this one, is already gone, just like that. And before I know it I'll be working out tonight, and then it'll be tomorrow and next week and next year, and college will be over, and it will all happen too quickly, not letting me savor it.

I realized, standing on the dock in the blackness with a white haze of galaxies above my head, that there is nothing to fear, nothing to worry about. I've loved so many things and so many people, and there have been many beautiful moments in my life. Beautiful songs and conversations.

How can I be bothered by running a mile in six minutes for college soccer when infinity is stretching out in front of me and telling me there are people on other worlds with the same feelings I have and that I can't even imagine how many other worlds there are, and that I'll die one day and who knows what'll happen after that?

It'll be a relief, sure, but life is exquisite and I've been able to experience a ton, and felt overwhelmed and crazy and enlightened over many things. If there were a way to know absolutely everything and not go crazy, I'd follow that path. I feel like the mind is too fragile to be able to do this, though. It's a sad thought.

There's something about observing things so much greater than oneself. Sublime.

03 August 2009

Davis and I hung out at a coffee shop till it closed, and then at a café for awhile. We've established that on Wednesday night we are going to get drunk at his house and play backgammon. I think I'm going to sleep there, but I'll tell my parents that I'm sleeping at Lisbet's because they'd get all weird if I said I was sleeping at Davis'. I don't know why I'm consenting to this because I know what will happen if we both get drunk… and I don't know if I want that to happen.

06 August 2009

Yesterday I ran a mile in five minutes and 52 seconds! Fucking crazy! The fastest I've ever gone. Then I told my parents I was going to sleep at Lisbet's house, and instead went to Davis'. Which was really weird. Like, we played backgammon and stuff and got pretty drunk, which was fine, but then we went on a walk in the dark with his dog, and he put his arm around me and was squeezing me the whole time, like I couldn't walk on my own or something. It was kind of annoying.

And yes, I'm just going to put it out there, we made out later. He's an okay kisser, I guess, but he wouldn't stop holding me and petting me like I was a fucking dog or something. You know how married people often sleep in each other's arms or, like, spoon? Well that is what he kept doing and it grossed me out.

He woke me up early before he had a dentist appointment and held and patted me for, like, 20 minutes. It was super irritating. I was like, I'm trying to sleep, get off me!! He's seriously obsessed with me, or something. He kept mentioning us hanging out over winter break and he was acting like we were dating. I'm glad I'm leaving for Seattle.

What sucks even more is that I left my water bottle cap over there so I have to see him again to get it. It would be pointless to try to explain to him that I don't really share his feelings since I'm leaving the day after tomorrow and I'm not going to see him ever. I feel super uncomfortable because he thinks I like him back and I actually don't. I just make out with whoever wants to make out with me when I am drunk. It's usually nothing sacred, you know?

07 August 2009

I'm leaving for Seattle tomorrow. Goodbye to this fucking shithole! I feel like finally I'm going to be a real person!

author's note

13 March 2020

What I really want to know is what kind of connection exists between mental states and perceptions, personal events, and the natal chart. I've given you the raw data. What can you tell me about the celestial bodies as archetypes, their relationships with each other in the natal chart as expressed through life context and circumstance, their energy forces and their transits through the houses and the signs?

I'm looking for conceptual and technical terms and explanations. You must back up your claims with evidence. Everything must relate to the data. I'd like you to assume that I know what you're talking about, that my comprehension is advanced, and that I understand your references.

What can you tell me about yin and yang, mirrors and messengers, "everything is everything"? What can you tell me about Ana, trapped in this time and dimension?

I'm asking for a love letter from the Universe, the All and Nothing, the Void as magic and unending.

I feel like I've finally found my meaning. To write, to be meta as fuck, to imbibe, to be analytical, strategic, strange, crazy on drugs that hand to me flashes of Uranium inspirations.

The thoughts I don't know how they're generated. I don't know how they come. It's only a type of mesmerization, something grabs me by the Spirit, something dangles unlimited opportunities in front of me and just out of reach, pointing me towards who I want to be.

All I want is to go to the Light like a moth, hypnotized by the force of Energy. Everything is your energy and your sense-states. Everything is a synthesis, you are in it, you are all it. Don't try to escape, learn to play the game of good Quality. Quality is King, is power, is courage, is justice and righteousness.

I am a slave to good, perfect, shimmering, irreal, subjective yet not, Quality. I want to be your muse, I want your Source as a reflection of my own. I want you to burn bright in me. I want to generate and transmit your fountain of Everything. I am a fucking portal, a satellite trapped in a woman's body.

I am Saturn's willing slave if he feeds me Divine, Sacred, Ephemeral Quality. I will do whatever the man with the scythe, the Father of Time, requires if he leads me towards the white Light at my center. If he lets me be the sage, if he hides concepts in symbols for me to follow frantically, for me to read as fast as I can. I will wait for eternity if he lets me be the most absorbent sponge psychologist, if he lets me passively view pencil lead spew grey onto a lined page, hypnotized by Energy possessing me as I filter it into words.

Is He doing this, the pragmatic scientist teacher, the reaper and Kronos? I am Him and He is Me. But maybe Pluto is the key.

I have figured out the Pattern but cannot yet Speak. They can only See you when you begin to See.

I want to dazzle you, bewilder you, befuddle you. I want to see the look on your face. I want you to do the same to me, to read my mind before I read yours, to dance out of my reach, to not give yourself up to me. I want to be the eternal chaser, the bedazzled, the one that is left with longing and solitude and repeating triple digits. Hints dropped into my consciousness.

I want the bouncing, hovering, black liquid at my center to merge with yours.

I want to play a game with you. I want to be your experiment, your astrological case study. I want you to tell me what I'm overlooking. I want you to be the Seer, the interpreter, the psychiatrist, the one who articulates prophecy. Where are you?

Best,
J. Guzmán

if you enjoyed this book

If you enjoyed this book I would love your feedback in the form of a short review. **Your comments are valuable and extremely appreciated, and will help me out on my indie author career path!!**

Follow me on Instagram @jguzmanwriter or visit my website jguzman.space. There you can sign up for my mailing list under the Contact tab.

Printed in Great Britain
by Amazon

77929814R00092